FOURTH EDITION

CONTENT AREA LEARNING
BRIDGES TO DISCIPLINARY LITERACY

Kendall Hunt
publishing company

**Includes
Common Core
Connections
and Technology
Applications**

Michael Manderino
Roberta L. Berglund
Jerry L. Johns

Book Team

Chairman and Chief Executive Officer   Mark C. Falb
President and Chief Operating Officer   Chad M. Chandlee
Vice President, Higher Education   David L. Tart
Director of Publishing Partnerships   Paul B. Carty
Senior Developmental Coordinator   Angela Willenbring
Project Coordinator   Charmayne McMurray
Permissions Editor   Caroline Kieler
Cover Designer   Heather Richman

Author Information for Correspondence and Workshops

Michael Manderino, Ph.D.
Assistant Professor of Literacy Education
Northern Illinois University
E-mail: *mmanderino@niu.edu*

Roberta L. Berglund, Ed.D.
Consultant in Reading/Language Arts
E-mail: *readboulder@yahoo.com*

Jerry L. Johns, Ph.D.
Consultant in Reading
E-mail: *jjohns@niu.edu*
Fax: 815-899-3022

Ordering Information

Address: Kendall Hunt Publishing Company
            4050 Westmark Drive
            Dubuque, IA 52004
Telephone: 800-247-3458, ext. 6
Website: www.kendallhunt.com
Fax: 800-772-9165

Kendall Hunt
publishing company

www.kendallhunt.com
Send all inquiries to:
4050 Westmark Drive
Dubuque, IA 52004-1840

Who Will Use This Book?

We have written this practical and useful book for a wide range of professionals in middle and high schools, including content area teachers and those working with students in literacy intervention support courses. This book is ideal for school, district, and other types of professional development programs. It will also be a helpful supplement in undergraduate and graduate reading and language arts classes as well as in clinical courses where there is a desire to provide useful strategies that have wide applicability and can be modified across the content areas. Professors teaching a content area/disciplinary literacy course will find the book especially valuable.

What Is New in This Edition?

The fourth edition of *Content Area Learning: Bridges to Disciplinary Literacy* has three notable additions. First, we address current scholarship that emphasizes *disciplinary literacy* (Moje, 2008; Shanahan & Shanahan, 2008, 2012). Disciplinary literacy is viewed as an approach to building content knowledge in particular disciplines as opposed to general strategies to be applied across disciplines. This book is intended to serve as a guide for teachers to bridge content area literacy strategies to the discipline-specific literacy strategies required to learn deeply in English Language Arts, Mathematics, Science, and History/Social Studies.

Second, we share ways that the strategies can be used to help students meet the demands of the Common Core State Standards (NGA Center & CCSSO, 2010). The Common Core State Standards were adopted in 2010 by 46 states and raise the level of reading demanded in each discipline. The Common Core State Standards provide distinct reading standards for English Language Arts, History/Social Studies, and Science and Technical Subjects. The strategies in this text align with the anchor Common Core State Standards and address the key shifts in the standards that include close reading, multiple text synthesis, comparative analysis, and text dependent comprehension.

Third, we provide ideas for implementing strategies using free web-based and iPad application technologies. As many schools and districts move toward 1:1 computing environments using a variety of technology platforms, the strategies presented here can be adapted for use with free Web 2.0 tools and/or iPad applications.

What Are Some of the Outstanding Qualities of This Book?

Content Area Learning: Bridges to Disciplinary Literacy contains 28 strategies. The strategies:

1. have specific connections to the Common Core State Standards.

2. have suggestions for technology integration so that they may be adapted in 1:1 environments.

3. address vocabulary, comprehension, multiple-text comprehension, and close reading.

4. are presented with a unique and helpful Quick Reference Guide that quickly shows Common Core State Standards and Disciplinary Considerations. The type of text (narrative or informational) with which the strategy can be used is also indicated.

5. are presented in an easy-to-follow, step-by-step manner.

6. contain one or more examples from the core content areas of English Language Arts, History/Social Studies, Math, and Science that are also part of the Common Core State Standards.

7. are accompanied, in almost all instances, by one or more reproducibles that you can use or adapt for student use.

What Insights Have Been Provided By Research?

A number of researchers in the field of literacy have focused on improving the literacy of adolescents by arguing that particular literacy practices are unique to each discipline (Moje, 2008; Shanahan & Shanahan, 2008). The comprehension of texts in a discipline is situated within these contexts. Rather than solely advocating the teaching of strategies for reading texts that can be applied across content areas, researchers advocate the teaching of discipline-specific strategies (Lee & Spratley, 2010; Moje, 2008; Shanahan & Shanahan, 2008, 2012). Shanahan and Shanahan (2008) argue that literacy demands become increasingly specialized when learning disciplinary content. While basic literacy processes are taught in earlier grades, teaching strategies in middle and high school often remain at the intermediate level (see Figure 1 below), where teachers spend a majority of instructional time teaching intermediate literacy strategies that don't always lead to more complex disciplinary learning.

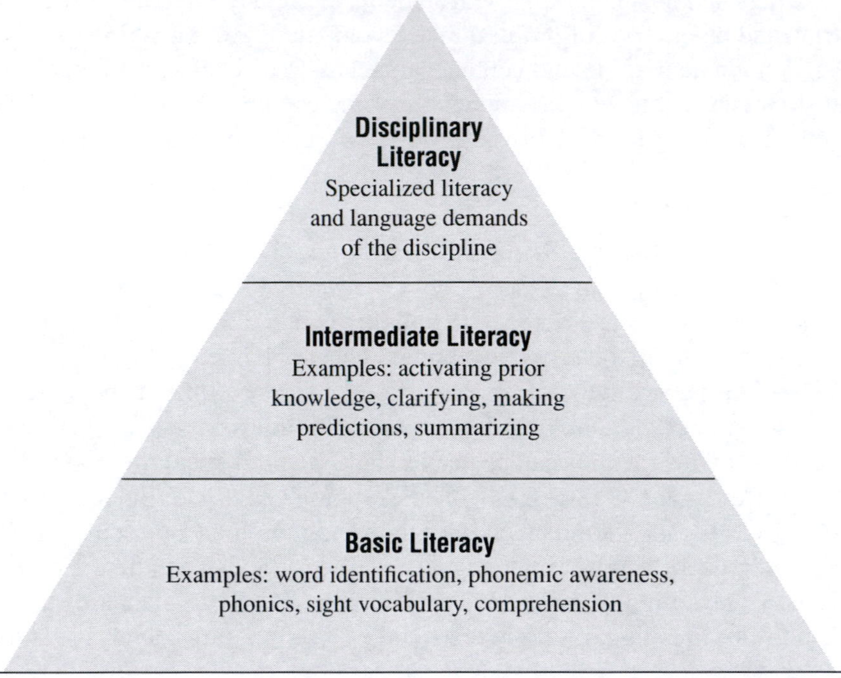

Disciplinary Literacy
Specialized literacy and language demands of the discipline

Intermediate Literacy
Examples: activating prior knowledge, clarifying, making predictions, summarizing

Basic Literacy
Examples: word identification, phonemic awareness, phonics, sight vocabulary, comprehension

Figure 1. Increasing Specialization of Literacy (adapted from Shanahan & Shanahan, 2008)

Examples of intermediate literacy strategies include activating prior knowledge, clarifying, making predictions, or summarizing. These strategic behaviors are embedded into what have been termed content area literacy strategies. Examples include the strategies that are provided in this text such as GIST, Possible Sentences, QARs, and Semantic Mapping.

One goal of this edition is to provide examples of how these types of intermediate literacy strategies can serve as a bridge to moving toward more discipline-specific literacy instruction. It has been established that there is an important relationship between literacy and learning in the content areas (Gray, 1925; Herber, 1970). Students must internalize the language of specific disciplines in order to think critically about the content. Unfortunately, studies have found that as content becomes more complex, student engagement with subject area reading declines significantly, most often by eighth grade (Gottfried, 1985). The National Assessment of Educational Progress (NAEP) scores also indicate a decline in reading performance in eighth grade (Grigg, Donahue, & Dion, 2007). These drops are related to a decrease in content area literacy instruction that encourages metacognition and deep reading (Guthrie & Davis, 2003).

Research on disciplinary literacy (Shanahan, Shanahan, & Misischia, 2011) analyzes how experts in the disciplines read and suggests that a one-size-fits-all approach is ineffective. Disciplinary experts use distinct literacy practices. For example, historians pay close attention to authorship and continuously juxtapose sources with one another (Wineburg, 1991). Scientists in the field of physics focus their attention on information they do not know and what information contradicts what they have previously thought about the topic (Bazerman, 1985). Each of these examples demonstrates that in order to read and learn from complex disciplinary texts, students need to engage in the habits of thinking used in the disciplines. Some researchers have thus defined disciplinary literacy in the following way:

> Disciplinary literacy involves the use of reading, reasoning, investigating, speaking, and writing required to learn and form complex content knowledge appropriate to a particular discipline. (McConachie & Petrosky, 2010, p. 16)

Consequently, content area instruction should use the primary disciplinary-literacy habits of thinking if students are to acquire deep content knowledge. Disciplinary literacy is an approach to building the requisite disciplinary knowledge required by a given domain. Disciplinary literacy entails the habits of practice valued in the disciplines and is comprised of 1) the habits of thinking used to make meaning; 2) a full range of texts and language use that shape thinking and practice; 3) the habits of practice enacted within the disciplines; and 4) the beliefs about knowledge and knowledge production that constitute the disciplines (Fang, 2012; Manderino, 2012; Moje, 2007, 2009; Shanahan & Shanahan, 2008; Wilson, 2011).

We agree that we need to move students toward these disciplinary habits, but they may still need support through the use of content area strategies (Fang & Coatoam, 2013). Students who lack conceptual knowledge and strategies in history, science, English language arts, or math to comprehend complex texts may be considered struggling adolescent readers (Alexander & Fox, 2011). As a result, explicit strategy instruction may be profitable for apprenticing disciplinary literacy instruction (Schoenbach, Greenleaf, & Murphy, 2012).

Disciplinary habits of reading, writing, talking, and thinking have also been delineated in the Common Core State Standards (CCSS) (NGA Center & CCSSO, 2010). The CCSS have been specifically written for the disciplines in grades 6–12. For the first time, literacy standards have been designed to treat reading, writing, talking, and thinking in the disciplines as distinct practices. These standards "**are meant to complement the specific content demands of the disciplines, not replace them**" (NGA Center & CCSSO, 2010, p. 60). As such, it is clear that students will need support to meet these discipline-specific literacy practices (Zygouris-Coe, 2012).

Content area literacy approaches have traditionally focused on more generalized reading processes such as summarization, predicting, questioning, and visualizing. These strategies are consistent with the report of the National Reading Panel (2000) that offered several strategies for effective comprehension instruction, including teaching students to summarize what they read. According to Cunningham (2001), the comprehension section of the National Reading Panel Report is potentially valuable. The following principles are generally consistent with two other major reviews (Pearson & Fielding, 1991; Tierney & Cunningham, 1984) and a related chapter (Pressley, 2000) of research on teaching comprehension.

1. Teach students to be aware of their own comprehension. This strategy is often referred to as comprehension monitoring or metacognition.

2. Have students work together on their strategies. This is referred to as cooperative learning.

3. Have students construct graphic summaries of what is read through the use of graphic and semantic organizers. Use them as a bridge to student-generated talk or writing.

4. Teach text structure.

5. Help students learn to ask and answer text-based questions.

6. Teach students to summarize what is read.

The strategies in this book are presented in a way to target more disciplinary-based reading/literacy strategies. Examples of disciplinary-based strategies according to the Wisconsin Department of Public Instruction (2012) include:

1. Building prior knowledge.

2. Building specialized vocabulary.

3. Learning to deconstruct complex sentences.

4. Using knowledge of text structures and genres to predict main and subordinate ideas.

5. Mapping graphic and mathematical representations against explanations in the text.

6. Posing discipline-relevant questions.

7. Comparing claims and propositions across texts.

8. Using norms for reasoning within the discipline (i.e., what counts as evidence) to evaluate claims.

Content area literacy strategies can serve as important scaffolds for disciplinary habits of reading, writing, talking, and thinking (Brozo, Moorman, Meyer, & Stewart, 2013). Explicit strategy instruction can provide students opportunities for learning and retaining content knowledge (Stahl & Fairbanks, 1986). Strategy instruction needs to be clearly explained, modeled, scaffolded, and aligned with disciplinary purposes for learning. However, to move toward a more discipline-specific habit of reading, students need to be guided to summarize for a particular disciplinary purpose. In history, one may summarize to connect key events in order to explain the causes and effects of a larger historical movement. In science, one might summarize to encapsulate critical steps in a scientific process. While it is clear that summarization is an effective strategy, it remains a more intermediate literacy strategy that needs to be focused in order to be effective with more complex disciplinary texts.

The strategies we provide are intended to be malleable. Shanahan (2012) argues that strategies can be general across disciplines (e.g., GIST, QARs); adaptable to meet disciplinary texts and tasks; or specific to a discipline, for example, Buehl's (2014) History Change Frame. The strategies we provide in this text are intended to be adaptable for use with different disciplinary texts and purposes. The strategies should help improve text comprehension within and across texts (Dole, Nokes, & Drits, 2009). Reproducibles are provided as initial models, but over time, students should be encouraged to begin to construct their own models to fit their tasks, texts, and reading goals. Ultimately, disciplinary-literacy strategies need to be contextualized and customized so that students can grapple with the literacy demands that are unique to the discipline. The strategies we offer can serve as a scaffold for students apprenticing into the disciplines. Like all scaffolds, the goal is to gradually fade the support as independence is gained. The strategies in this text are an initial step toward disciplinary literacy but not a final destination in terms of acquiring disciplinary literacy. The strategies in this book provide discipline-specific adaptations for English language arts, social studies, science, and math.

The key ingredients, however, are your actions as a teacher. You can help students set discipline-specific goals and provide explicit strategy instruction for reaching those disciplinary goals. Consider the following gradual-release model in Figure 2 (page vii) based on Pearson and Gallagher (1983) and adapted from Buehl (2014) and the Wisconsin Department of Public Instruction (2012).

- Tell students the goals for learning in the discipline.
- Tell students how the strategies promote disciplinary learning.
- Model the habits of reading, writing, talking, and thinking in the discipline.
- Model how the strategies are used to promote those disciplinary habits.
- Think aloud by describing what goes on in your mind while you are using the strategy.
- Gradually release responsibility to students.
- Provide guided practice so students can learn how the strategy will help them understand the content.
- Reinforce student efforts.
- Develop the strategies over time and remind students to use the strategies as needed.
- Have students reflect on the strategies and how they help in particular contexts.

Figure 2 is an example of the gradual release of responsibility in the context of disciplinary-literacy instruction. The model represents the scaffolding and support needed to engage students in constructing disciplinary knowledge. As guided practices fade, student ownership of both intermediate and disciplinary strategies increases. The goal is for students to use disciplinary-literacy strategies to construct meaning. To achieve that end, teachers can create classroom activities that engage students in direct strategy instruction as well as apprenticing them into discipline-specific habits of reading, writing, thinking, and speaking through collaborative inquiry. Over time, student meaning-making should become increasingly discipline-specific using disciplinary-literacy strategies that are relevant and appropriate.

We want to stress again the critical importance of teaching the strategies for specific disciplinary purposes. The intermediate strategies in this book are intended to help move students towards the acquisition and independent use of disciplinary literacy strategies.

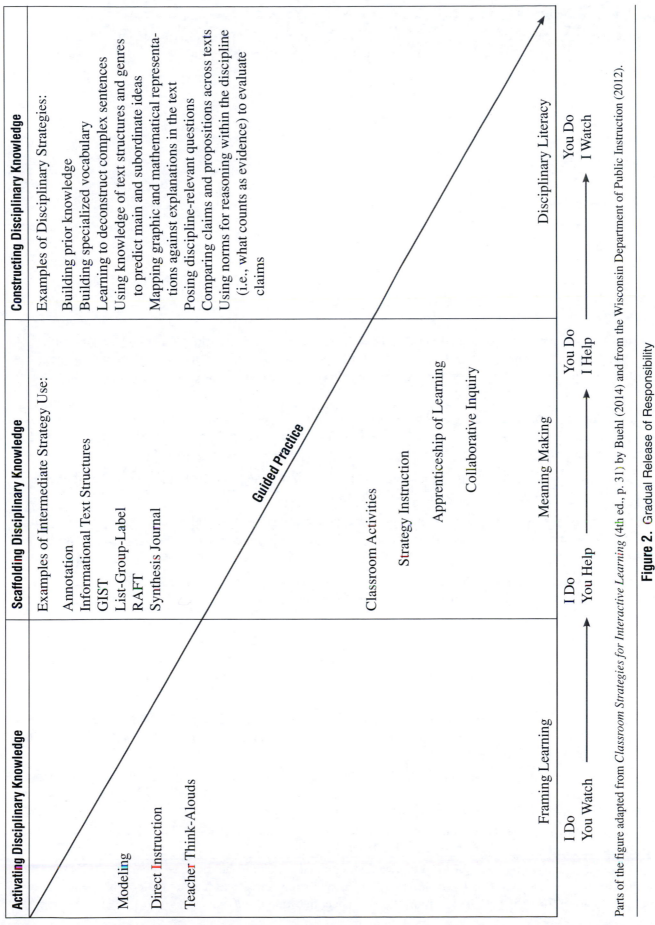

Activating Disciplinary Knowledge	Scaffolding Disciplinary Knowledge	Constructing Disciplinary Knowledge
	Examples of Intermediate Strategy Use:	Examples of Disciplinary Strategies:
	Annotation	Building prior knowledge
	Informational Text Structures	Building specialized vocabulary
	GIST	Learning to deconstruct complex sentences
Modeling	List-Group-Label	Using knowledge of text structures and genres to predict main and subordinate ideas
Direct Instruction	RAFT	Mapping graphic and mathematical representations against explanations in the text
Teacher Think-Alouds	Synthesis Journal	Posing discipline-relevant questions
		Comparing claims and propositions across texts
		Using norms for reasoning within the discipline (i.e., what counts as evidence) to evaluate claims

Guided Practice

Classroom Activities

Strategy Instruction

Apprenticeship of Learning

Collaborative Inquiry

Framing Learning	Meaning Making	Disciplinary Literacy
I Do You Watch →	I Do You Help →	You Do I Help →
	You Do I Watch →	

Figure 2. Gradual Release of Responsibility

Parts of the figure adapted from *Classroom Strategies for Interactive Learning* (4th ed., p. 31) by Buehl (2014) and from the Wisconsin Department of Public Instruction (2012).

What Are the Key Features of This Book?

The format and organization of this book make it very user-friendly. We have included a Quick Reference Guide inside the front cover so you can easily locate the various strategies and consider their best use. The book is organized by the following categories:

Description

Bridge to the Disciplines

Technology Connections

Text Type

Disciplinary Considerations

Common Core Anchor Standards

Strategic Behaviors

Suggested Uses for Disciplinary Literacy

Description indicates the roots of the strategy and its overall purposes from a content area literacy perspective. For example, Save the Last Word for Me is described as a useful strategy for facilitating text-based discussion in the disciplines.

Bridge to the Disciplines provides a rationale for how the strategy might be adapted to match your disciplinary instructional goals. For example, Save the Last Word for Me provides an opportunity for students to engage in close/critical disciplinary reading, like interrogating the author's claims and the use of evidence to support those claims.

Technology Connections offer practical suggestions for adapting the strategies for use with 1:1 devices such as laptops and/or iPads. For example, Save the Last Word for Me can be used with online platforms like www.quizlet.com or www.todaysmeet.com.

Text Type refers to the two major classifications of materials: narrative and informational text. For example, Save the Last Word for Me can be used with both types of text.

Disciplinary Considerations are based on disciplinary literacy strategies like building prior knowledge, building specialized vocabulary, and using norms for reasoning within the discipline (i.e., what counts as evidence) to evaluate claims.

Common Core Anchor Standards indicate the anchor reading, writing, language, and speaking and listening standards that can best be addressed through the use of the strategy. Save the Last Word for Me is best aligned with two anchor reading standards.

Strategic Behaviors are based on Duke and Pearson (2002), Keene (2008), Keene and Zimmermann (1997), Pearson, Roehler, Dole, and Duffy (1992), and others who have conducted and reviewed the research in comprehension. These strategies help students become thoughtful, independent readers who are engaged in their reading and learning. The following are brief descriptions of the strategic behaviors we use in this book:

- *Monitoring Meaning*—Students who monitor meaning as they read know that the text should make sense to them. If not, they use fix-up strategies such as pausing, rereading, and/or discussing their understanding with others to help clarify meaning.

- *Using Prior Knowledge*—Students use their background knowledge before, during, and after reading to make sense of and remember new information. They assimilate new information into their background knowledge. This is sometimes referred to as using and developing their schema.

- *Asking Questions*—Students generate questions before, during, and after reading. They use their questions to help them focus and remember important ideas from the text.

- *Inferring*—Students combine their prior knowledge with that which is read to create meaning that is not explicitly stated in the text. Readers who infer, draw conclusions, make and revise predictions, use and interpret information from the text, make connections, answer questions, and make judgments about the reading.

- *Creating Images*—Using all five senses and their emotions, students create images during and after reading. They may use their images to make connections, recall, and interpret details from the reading.

- *Determining Importance*—As they read, students make decisions about what they believe is important in the text. These might be words, sentences, or main ideas developed from the reading. They then draw conclusions about the key ideas or major concepts contained in the text.

- *Synthesizing*—Students put together information from the text, information from other relevant sources, and their background knowledge to create understanding of what has been read. Students use text structures and text elements as they read to predict, confirm or reject ideas, assimilate thoughts, and create overall meaning. "A synthesis is the sum of information from the text, other relevant texts, and the reader's background knowledge . . . produced in an original way" (Keene, 2008, p. 252).

You can see that Save the Last Word for Me helps with *using prior knowledge, asking questions, inferring, determining importance,* and *synthesizing.*

Suggested Uses for Disciplinary Literacy include specific instructional ideas for using a strategy to help students access complex disciplinary texts (Buehl, 2011) and use those texts to build disciplinary knowledge. Buehl (2011) argues that:

> Generic strategies can be understood as instructional prototypes, as models that illustrate how literacy practices can be embedded into disciplinary learning. However, prototypes are only starting points. Such practices will need to be fine-tuned and even reconfigured as teachers examine how generic literacy strategies can be customized to fit the unique demands of texts in their disciplines. (pp. 266–267)

Save the Last Word for Me can be used in English Language Arts (ELA), Social Studies, Science, and Math, but is used for different purposes based on disciplinary goals and norms. As Hynd-Shanahan (2013) suggests, you should lead with your disciplinary texts and tasks and then select and adapt the strategy. These are simply initial ideas for using these strategies in specific disciplinary contexts. We encourage you to identify your disciplinary goals and then adapt the strategies offered in this text as needed.

Sample Save the Last Word for Me for **Psychology**

Directions: As you read, make a light mark with your pencil next to three statements in the text that *represent important steps in the process* of Coping with Loss. When you finish reading, write each statement in one of the boxes below. Then write your reasoning for choosing that statement. You might include questions or personal connections you have as well. When you finish, you will have the opportunity to discuss the text with a small group of your classmates.

Title: _Coping with Loss_

My first quote, page _228_

Any loss requires change and that change can be stressful.

My reasoning for selecting this quote:

An important part of the process is recognizing that change will occur. One needs to expect that loss will cause stress.

My second quote, page _229_

Hope operates through all five stages of grief.

My reasoning for selecting this quote:

There are five stages of grief. Hope is an important part of each stage.

My third quote, page _230_

What helped me most was talking to my family.

My reasoning for selecting this quote:

Talking is an important part of the process for coping with loss. Other important parts of the process include acceptance and seeking the comfort of others.

References

Alexander, P. A., & Fox, E. (2011). Adolescents as readers. In M. L. Kamil, P. D. Pearson, E. B. Moje, & P. P. Afflerbach (Eds.), (2010), *Handbook of reading research* (Vol. 4, pp. 157–176). New York, NY: Routledge.

Bazerman, C. (1985). Physicists reading physics: Schema-laden purposes and purpose-laden schema. *Written Communication, 2*(1), 3–23.

Brozo, W. G., Moorman, G., Meyer, C., & Stewart, T. (2013). Content area reading and disciplinary literacy: A case for the radical center. *Journal of Adolescent & Adult Literacy, 56,* 353–357.

Buehl, D. (2011). *Developing readers in the academic disciplines.* Newark, DE: International Reading Association.

Buehl, D. (2014). *Classroom strategies for interactive learning* (4th ed.). Newark, DE: International Reading Association.

Cunningham, J. W. (2001). The National Reading Panel Report. (Essay Book Review). *Reading Research Quarterly, 36,* 326–335.

Dole, J., Nokes, J., & Drits, D. (2009). Cognitive strategy instruction. In G. Duffy & S. Israel (Eds.), *Handbook of research on reading comprehension* (pp. 347–372). Mahwah, NJ: Erlbaum.

Duke, N., & Pearson, P. D. (2002). Effective practices for developing reading comprehension. In A. E. Farstrup & S. J. Samuels (Eds.), *What research has to say about reading instruction* (3rd ed., pp. 205–242). Newark, DE: International Reading Association.

Fang, Z. (2012). Language correlates of disciplinary literacy. *Topics in Language Disorders, 32,* 19–34.

Fang, Z., & Coatoam, S. (2013). Disciplinary literacy: What you want to know about it. *Journal of Adolescent & Adult Literacy, 56,* 627–632.

Gottfried, A. E. (1985). Academic intrinsic motivation in elementary and junior high school students. *Journal of Educational Psychology, 77,* 631–645.

Gray, W. S. (1925). Reading activities in school and in social life. In G. M. Whipple (Ed.), *The twenty-fourth yearbook of the National Society for the Study of Education, Part I* (pp. 1–8). Bloomington, IL: Public School Publishing.

Grigg, W., Donahue, P., & Dion, G. (2007). *The nation's report card: 12th-grade reading and mathematics 2005* (NCES 2007-468). U.S. Department of Education, National Center for Education Statistics. Washington, DC: U.S. Government Printing Office.

Guthrie, J. T., & Davis, M. H. (2003). Motivating struggling readers in middle school through an engagement model of classroom practice. *Reading & Writing Quarterly, 19,* 59–85.

Herber, H. L. (1970). *Teaching reading in the content areas.* Englewood Cliffs, NJ: Prentice Hall.

Hynd-Shanahan, C. (2013). What does it take? *Journal of Adolescent & Adult Literacy, 57,* 93–98.

Keene, E. O. (2008). *To understand: New horizons in reading comprehension.* Portsmouth, NH: Heinemann.

Keene, E. O., & Zimmermann, S. (1997). *Mosaic of thought.* Portsmouth, NH: Heinemann.

Lee, C. D., & Spratley, A. (2010). *Reading in the disciplines: The challenges of adolescent literacy.* New York, NY: Carnegie Corporation of New York.

Manderino, M. (2012). Disciplinary literacy in new literacies environments: Expanding the intersections of literate practice for adolescents. In P. J. Dunston, L. B. Gambrell, S. King Fullerton, K. Headley, & P. M. Stecker (Eds.), *61st yearbook of the Literacy Research Association* (pp. 69–83). Oak Creek, WI: Literacy Research Association.

McConachie, S. M., & Petrosky, A. R. (2010). *Content matters: A disciplinary literacy approach to improving student learning.* San Francisco, CA: Jossey-Bass.

Moje, E. B. (2007). Developing socially just subject-matter instruction: A review of the literature on disciplinary literacy teaching. *Review of Research in Education 2007, 31,* 1–44.

Moje, E. B. (2008). Foregrounding the disciplines in secondary literacy teaching and learning: A call for change. *Journal of Adolescent & Adult Literacy, 52,* 96–107.

Moje, E. B. (2009). A call for new research on new and multi-literacies. *Research in the Teaching of English, 43,* 348–362.

National Governors Association Center for Best Practices & Council of Chief State School Officers (NGA Center & CCSSO). (2010). *Common Core State Standards for English language arts and literacy in history/social studies, science, and technical subjects.* Washington, DC: Authors.

National Reading Panel. (2000). *Teaching children to read: An evidence-based assessment of the scientific research literature on reading and its implications for reading instruction.* Washington, DC: National Institute for Child Health and Human Development.

Pearson, P. D., & Fielding, L. (1991). Comprehension instruction. In R. Barr, M. L. Kamil, P. B. Mosenthal, & P. D. Pearson (Eds.), *Handbook of reading research* (Vol. 2, pp. 815–816). White Plains, NY: Longman.

Pearson, P. D., & Gallagher, M. C. (1983). The instruction of reading comprehension. *Contemporary Educational Psychology, 8,* 317–344.

Pearson, P. D., Roehler, L. R., Dole, J. A., & Duffy, G. G. (1992). Developing expertise in reading comprehension. In S. J. Samuels & A. E. Farstrup (Eds.), *What research has to say about reading instruction* (2nd ed., pp. 145–199). Newark, DE: International Reading Association.

Pressley, M. (2000). What should comprehension instruction be the instruction of? In M. L. Kamil, P. B. Mosenthal, P. D. Pearson, & R. Barr (Eds.), *Handbook of reading research* (Vol. 3, pp. 545–561). Mahwah, NJ: Erlbaum.

Schoenbach, R., Greenleaf, C., & Murphy, L. (2012). *Reading for understanding: How Reading Apprenticeship improves disciplinary learning in secondary and college classrooms.* Hoboken, NJ: Wiley.

Shanahan, C. (2012). How disciplinary experts read. In T. L. Jetton & C. Shanahan (Eds.), *Adolescent literacy in the academic disciplines: General principles and practical strategies* (pp. 69–90). New York, NY: Guilford.

Shanahan, C., Shanahan, T., & Misischia, C. (2011). Analysis of expert readers in three disciplines: History, mathematics, and chemistry. *Journal of Literacy Research, 43,* 393–429.

Shanahan, T., & Shanahan, C. (2008). Teaching disciplinary literacy to adolescents: Rethinking content-area literacy. *Harvard Education Review, 78,* 40–61.

Shanahan, T., & Shanahan, C. (2012). What is disciplinary literacy and why does it matter? *Topics in Language Disorders, 32*, 7–18.

Stahl, S. A., & Fairbanks, M. (1986). The effects of vocabulary instruction: A model based meta-analysis. *Review of Education Research, 56*, 72–110.

Tierney, R. J., & Cunningham, J. W. (1984). Research on teaching reading comprehension. In P. D. Pearson, R. Barr, M. L. Kamil, & P. Mosenthal (Eds.), *Handbook of reading research* (Vol. 1, pp. 609–655). White Plains, NY: Longman.

Wilson, A. (2011). A social semiotics framework for conceptualizing content area literacies. *Journal of Adolescent & Adult Literacy, 54*, 435–444.

Wineburg, S. S. (1991). Historical problem solving: A study of the cognitive processes used in evaluation of documentary and pictorial evidence. *Journal of Educational Psychology, 83*, 73–87.

Wisconsin Department of Public Instruction. (2012). *Literacy in the discipline and disciplinary literacy: A place for both.* Retrieved from http://standards.dpi.wi.gov/files/cal/pdf/literacy-disciplines.pdf

Zygouris-Coe, V. (2012). Disciplinary literacy and the Common Core State Standards. *Topics in Language Disorders, 32*, 35–50.

Michael Manderino is an assistant professor of literacy education at Northern Illinois University. He is a former high school social studies teacher of 14 years. Additionally, he acted as a district literacy coordinator and literacy coach for two years, and he and his colleagues implemented a district-wide disciplinary literacy initiative. Michael earned his Ph.D. in Literacy, Language, and Culture from the University of Illinois at Chicago in 2011. He was the recipient of the Outstanding Student Research Award for his dissertation from the Literacy Research Association, received the Outstanding Dissertation Award from the Association of Literacy Educators and Researchers, and was a finalist for the Outstanding Dissertation Award from the International Reading Association. Michael's research interests center around the intersection of disciplinary literacy and multi-literacies at the secondary level. His research investigates how students process multiple texts in discipline-specific contexts with multimedia texts. He also researches the impact of high school literacy coaching.

Roberta L. (Bobbi) Berglund has received honors for outstanding service throughout her career, which includes serving as a classroom teacher, reading specialist, ELL resource teacher, director of Title I programs, and director of literacy. Dr. Berglund has also been a member of the reading faculty at the University of Wisconsin-Whitewater and has taught undergraduate and graduate reading courses at Northern Illinois University, Rockford University, National Louis University, and Aurora University. Dr. Berglund has worked with school districts and state education agencies in developing curriculum materials, assessments, and leading professional development programs. She has been a speaker at state, national, and international conferences and a leader in professional organizations. Dr. Berglund is the author of over 50 publications and is the author or coauthor of 15 professional books.

Jerry L. Johns has been recognized as a distinguished teacher, writer, outstanding teacher educator, and professional development speaker for schools, school districts, and conferences. He has taught students from kindergarten through graduate school and also served as a reading teacher. Professor Johns spent his career at Northern Illinois University. He served in leadership positions at the local, state, national, and international levels. He has been president of the International Reading Association, the Illinois Reading Council, the Association of Literacy Educators and Researchers, and the Northern Illinois Reading Council. He also served on the board of directors for each of these organizations, as well as the American Reading Forum. Dr. Johns has authored or co-authored nearly 300 articles, monographs, and research studies as well as numerous professional books. His *Basic Reading Inventory*, now in the 11th edition, is widely used in undergraduate and graduate classes as well as by practicing teachers.

Annotation
(Bookmarks, SMART, Sticky Notes, Text Coding)

Description

Text annotation is a reading and writing strategy that encourages students to note important ideas, connections, and examples in the margins of a text (Brown, 2007; Nist & Hogrebe, 1987; Porter-O'Donnell, 2004). Annotation offers opportunities for students to engage deeply with the text, use active reading techniques, and talk to the text (Porter-O'Donnell, 2004). Annotations can take several forms, including Bookmarks, SMART, Sticky Notes, or Text Coding. Procedures for each technique are provided on pages 2–10 as well as reproducibles and examples.

Bridge to the Disciplines

While annotation provides opportunities for metacognitive processing of a text, it also is an important part of noting crucial elements about how a disciplinary text functions. As the purposes for reading a text vary by discipline, so do the purposes for marking the text. Explicit instruction in annotation techniques can provide support for close reading of disciplinary texts and opportunities for students to develop their own annotation methods.

Technology Connections

A text can be annotated in Microsoft Word or in a PDF by adding sticky notes or comment boxes. Platforms like Evernote also have functions to annotate, and www.diigo.com is a Web 2.0 app for annotating websites; iPad applications such as Notability and iAnnotate are perhaps most widely used for digital annotations.

Text Type
Narrative
Informational

Disciplinary Considerations
- Close reading
- Building prior knowledge
- Building specialized vocabulary

Common Core Anchor Standards
Reading
- Read closely to determine what the text says explicitly and to make logical inferences from it; cite specific textual evidence when writing or speaking to support conclusions drawn from the text.
- Analyze the structure of texts, including how specific sentences, paragraphs, and larger portions of the text (e.g., a section, chapter, scene, or stanza) relate to each other and the whole.

Writing
- Draw evidence from literary or informational texts to support analysis, reflection, and research.

Strategic Behaviors
Using Prior Knowledge
Asking Questions
Inferring
Determining Importance
Synthesizing

Suggested Uses for Disciplinary Literacy
ELA: Have students mark the text for author's use of figurative language.

History: Have students mark the text for evidence of historical significance.

Science: Have students note key parts of a scientific process.

Math: Have students mark problem sets to identify key elements to be solved.

References

Brown, M. D. (2007). I'll have mine annotated, please: Helping students make connections with texts. *English Journal, 96*(4), 73–78.

Nist, S. L., & Hogrebe, M. C. (1987). The role of underlining and annotating in remembering textual information. *Literacy Research and Instruction, 27*, 12–25.

Porter-O'Donnell, C. (2004). Beyond the yellow highlighter: Teaching annotation skills to improve reading comprehension. *English Journal, 93*(5), 82–89.

Bookmarks

Description

Bookmarks (Beers, 2003; Daniels & Zemelman, 2004) give students a place to record their thoughts while reading. When students record their thoughts on the Bookmarks, they become active readers who make connections, ask questions, and determine important ideas. Bookmarks can also be used for recording key concepts or vocabulary words that are significant to the reading.

Procedure

1. Duplicate and distribute copies of the Bookmarks reproducible on page 3. Have students fold the reproducible in half.

2. Select an excerpt from a text that students will be asked to read.

3. Read a portion of the text aloud and model what kinds of thoughts can be recorded on Bookmarks. Try to provide examples that include a variety of responses: personal connections, questions, important passages, and key vocabulary.

4. Have students continue reading from the text and record their thoughts on the Bookmarks as they read. An example follows.

Sample Bookmarks for **Social Studies**

Name: _Amy_

Topic: _Louisiana Purchase_

—Robert Livingston and James Monroe negotiated the purchase.
—What would have happened if Napoleon decided not to sell the Louisiana Territory?
—I think at the time, $15 million was a lot of money for the purchase. The aftermath of Hurricane Katrina will cost much more.
—How much land did the U.S. actually acquire?

Name: _Amy_

Topic: _Louisiana Purchase_

Vocabulary Word: _cede_

Page _362_

to grant or give up land

Vocabulary Word: _Louisiana Territory_

Page _362_

Land from the Mississippi River west to the Rocky Mountains

5. Invite students to discuss their responses with a partner or in collaborative groups.

6. Encourage whole-group sharing to identify the range and variety of responses students recorded while reading.

7. Bookmarks can also be used after reading to help students recall their understanding of the selected text.

References

Beers, K. (2003). *When kids can't read: What teachers can do*. Portsmouth, NH: Heinemann.
Daniels, H., & Zemelman, S. (2004). *Subjects matter: Every teacher's guide to content-area reading*. Portsmouth, NH: Heinemann.

Bookmarks

Name: _____

Topic: _____

Name: _____

Topic: _____

Vocabulary Word: _____

Page _____

Vocabulary Word: _____

Page _____

Vocabulary Word: _____

Page _____

Vocabulary Word: _____

Page _____

Vocabulary Word: _____

Page _____

Self-Monitoring Approach to Reading and Thinking (SMART)

Description

The Self-Monitoring Approach to Reading and Thinking (SMART) (Buehl, 2014; Vaughan & Estes, 1986) is a strategy that encourages students to develop an awareness of what they do and do not understand as they read. This self-monitoring strategy helps students think about their reading to be more aware of how it is proceeding. Students use a notation system during reading and a variety of fix-up strategies for difficult portions of the text. They also evaluate the usefulness of the strategies, thereby enhancing their metacognition (awareness of one's own learning).

Procedure

1. Find a passage consisting of several paragraphs that is somewhat challenging for you. The passage may need to be enlarged for effective viewing by students.

2. Read the first few sentences of the passage. If it makes sense to you, place a check mark (✓) in the margin and say something like, "This makes sense to me. I feel like I really understand it." If it seems confusing, place a question mark (?) in the margin and say something like, "I'm not sure what this means. Maybe as I read on I will understand it better."

3. Continue modeling the use of the check mark (✓) and question mark (?) and comment on your reasons for using the marking system. You might say, "These marks will help me think about my reading and how well I am understanding what I am reading. Good readers know when they aren't understanding something, and they also know when they should try something else when they don't understand."

4. After completing the modeled reading for students, look at each question mark (?) and talk with students about how to make sense of those parts of the text. Sometimes just rereading the text helps the reader understand. If this is the case for you, change the question mark (?) to a check mark (✓) in the margin. For other question-marked sections, talk about the problem. Why is the section difficult to understand? Is it the vocabulary? Is the language confusing? Do you know very little about the topic?

5. Ask students for their ideas of ways to help the text make sense. List these ideas as students offer them. Suggestions might be to paraphrase the text, use pictures, charts, or graphs to give clues to understanding, check the glossary or other references to determine the meaning of unknown or difficult words, look at other parts of the text such as the summary and review sections, and ask a teacher or another classmate for help. Take time to discuss how the various strategies may provide clues to help construct meaning.

6. Introduce the passage students will be reading. Tell students to use a pencil to lightly mark the text using the check mark (✓) and question (?) system to help them monitor the reading.

7. Make copies of the SMART Strategy Log reproducible on page 6. After students have read and marked the passages, have them work with a partner and discuss the sections marked with question marks (?). Have them use the SMART Strategy Log to record their reading processes. Remind students that if the problem is "something else," there is space provided to write it.

8. After completing the SMART Strategy Log, discuss with students the strategies that help them work through problems with a text. Review or teach what they need to do when they don't understand what they are reading in subsequent lessons.

9. Have students complete the SMART Strategy Log from time to time to make them more aware of ways to monitor their comprehension. A completed SMART example is found on page 5.

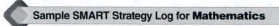

Sample SMART Strategy Log for **Mathematics**

Directions: After reading, find the page and paragraph of each question mark (?) in the margin of your text. Write them under the *Page/Paragraph* headings. Then look at each section of the text marked with a question mark (?). Ask yourself, *What's the Problem?* Check (✓) the things that may be problems or write your problem on the lines. Then try some fix-up strategies. Check (✓) those that you tried under the *What I Tried* column. Then think about how each strategy worked. Mark your responses in the *How It Worked* column with a check mark.

Page/Paragraph with "?"	What's the Problem?	What I Tried	How It Worked
	✓ Difficult Word	✓ Glossary	Great! I Get It!
	Confusing Sentence	Reread Text	✓ It Helped
	Don't Know Much About It	Pictures/Graphics	OK
36 / 3		Summarize	Not Much Help
	_____	Review Section	
		Diagrams	
	_____	✓ Ask Someone	
		Something Else _____	

Page/Paragraph with "?"	What's the Problem?	What I Tried	How It Worked
	Difficult Word	Glossary	✓ Great! I Get It!
	✓ Confusing Sentence	✓ Reread Text	It Helped
	Don't Know Much About It	Pictures/Graphics	OK
38 / 1		Summarize	Not Much Help
	_____	Review Section	
		Diagrams	
	_____	Ask Someone	
		Something Else _____	

Additional Considerations for Successful Implementation

♦ After multiple practices, encourage students to add written annotations next to their check marks (✓) and questions (?). Ultimately, students should develop their own system for monitoring their reading.

© legenda, 2014. Under license from Shutterstock, Inc.

References

Buehl, D. (2014). *Classroom strategies for interactive learning* (4th ed.). Newark, DE: International Reading Association.

Vaughan, J. L., & Estes, T. H. (1986). *Reading and reasoning beyond the primary grades*. Boston, MA: Allyn & Bacon.

SMART Strategy Log

Directions: After reading, find the page and paragraph of each question mark (?) in the margin of your text. Write them under the *Page/Paragraph* headings. Then look at each section of the text marked with a question mark (?). Ask yourself, *What's the Problem?* Check (✔) the things that may be problems or write your problem on the lines. Then try some fix-up strategies. Check (✔) those that you tried under the *What I Tried* column. Then think about how each strategy worked. Mark your responses in the *How It Worked* column with a check mark.

Page/Paragraph with "?"	*What's the Problem?*	*What I Tried*	*How It Worked*
	Difficult Word	Glossary	Great! I Get It!
	Confusing Sentence	Reread Text	It Helped
	Don't Know Much About It	Pictures/Graphics	OK
____ / ____		Summarize	Not Much Help
	_____	Review Section	
		Diagrams	
	_____	Ask Someone	
		Something Else _____	

Page/Paragraph with "?"	*What's the Problem?*	*What I Tried*	*How It Worked*
	Difficult Word	Glossary	Great! I Get It!
	Confusing Sentence	Reread Text	It Helped
	Don't Know Much About It	Pictures/Graphics	OK
		Summarize	Not Much Help
____ / ____	_____	Review Section	
		Diagrams	
	_____	Ask Someone	
		Something Else _____	

Page/Paragraph with "?"	*What's the Problem?*	*What I Tried*	*How It Worked*
	Difficult Word	Glossary	Great! I Get It!
	Confusing Sentence	Reread Text	It Helped
	Don't Know Much About It	Pictures/Graphics	OK
		Summarize	Not Much Help
____ / ____	_____	Review Section	
		Diagrams	
	_____	Ask Someone	
		Something Else _____	

Page/Paragraph with "?"	*What's the Problem?*	*What I Tried*	*How It Worked*
	Difficult Word	Glossary	Great! I Get It!
	Confusing Sentence	Reread Text	It Helped
	Don't Know Much About It	Pictures/Graphics	OK
		Summarize	Not Much Help
____ / ____	_____	Review Section	
		Diagrams	
	_____	Ask Someone	
		Something Else _____	

Sticky Notes

Description

Sticky Notes (Daniels & Zemelman, 2004; Harvey & Goudvis, 2007; Hoyt, 2002) encourage students to monitor their thinking while reading by jotting down brief notes and sticking them on the pages of the text that prompted their thoughts. Students can jot down brief comments, write questions, make predictions and connections, or mark an interesting phrase or sentence in the text. Sticky Notes become a record of students' thinking that can later be used for review, discussion, and assessment.

Procedure

1. Choose a passage from a text to read aloud and provide copies or display it so that students can follow along with you. Explain that you will be stopping while reading to write down your thinking on Sticky Notes.

2. Begin reading the text aloud and stop at a point where you can share a personal connection, ask a question, make a prediction, or note the author's use of language. On a Sticky Note, write down your prediction; read it aloud to students, then place it on the page to mark the spot in the text to show your thinking. Continue reading and stop to share your written thoughts on Sticky Notes.

3. As you continue reading aloud, elicit students' thoughts. Model how to jot down their responses on the Sticky Notes using a chart, LCD projector, or SMART Board.

4. After modeling several examples, provide time for students to practice individually by recording their thinking on Sticky Notes.

5. Invite students to share their Sticky Notes with a partner or use them in a whole-class discussion. You might ask students to place their Sticky Notes on chart paper after reading a selection of text or use the reproducible on page 8. Responses can be organized into like categories and used to engage students in discussion. Possible categories might include predictions, connections, questions, visualizations, summaries, judgments, and interesting passages.

6. With informational text, you can demonstrate how to mark a photo or illustration in the text with a question.

7. Upon completing the reading, students should have a collection of Sticky Notes that can be stored in a notebook for later discussion and review.

Additional Considerations for Successful Implementation

- After multiple practices, encourage students to add information to their Sticky Notes upon rereading a text.
- Have students reorganize their Sticky Notes after reading new texts about the topic or at the end of the unit.

References

Daniels, H., & Zemelman, S. (2004). *Subjects matter: Every teacher's guide to content-area reading*. Portsmouth, NH: Heinemann.
Harvey, S., & Goudvis, A. (2007). *Strategies that work* (2nd ed.). Portland, ME: Stenhouse.
Hoyt, L. (2002). *Make it real: Strategies for success with informational texts*. Portsmouth, NH: Heinemann.

Sticky Notes Record Sheet

Title _____

My Predictions	My Questions

My Connections	My Evaluation

My Summary	

Text Coding

Description

Good readers conduct active conversations in their heads by reacting to, questioning, and synthesizing information as they read. All readers can be helped to become more aware of their thinking and engaged in the reading process. One method for doing so is Text Coding (Harvey & Goudvis, 2007; Tovani, 2000; Vaughan & Estes, 1986). Using a simple coding system, students make notations in the margins of the text or on sticky notes to encourage them to monitor their comprehension as they read. Text Codes can increase in number and complexity depending on the students' maturity, comfort, and experience in using them. By using Text Codes, students are scaffolded to think critically as they read the assigned material and are more prepared to discuss their thoughts and reactions with others.

Procedure

1. Select reading material and display it for students to see.

2. Read a portion of the text aloud, modeling how proficient readers carry on internal conversations in their heads as they read. Highlight, underline, or make comments on the displayed text that reflect your thoughts.

3. After modeling several think-alouds for students, introduce a few simple Text Codes. Show how underlining and highlighting can be replaced with a marginal notation or sticky note containing an * (very important information; key concept; new information), a ? (confusing information; something doesn't make sense; question), a ✓ (something you already knew), or an ! (something you find interesting, hard to believe, or unexpected).

4. Provide students with text material that can be written on or give them small sticky notes to use for their codes. Invite students to read the material and use the codes to track their thinking. You may wish to provide copies of the reproducible on page 10 and have students highlight specific codes that you want them to use. Start with a small number of codes and increase them as needed.

5. After students have coded the text, invite them to discuss their reactions with a partner.

6. As students become more experienced with coding as they read, form discussion groups of five or six students. Select a discussion leader to compose questions for the group to discuss. Each student in the group is responsible to share their Text Coding as evidence they have carefully engaged in their reading.

7. When groups come together, the discussion leader facilitates the conversation about the texts and all students participate, using their coded material as the basis of their comments.

8. As students become more proficient using Text Coding, encourage them to generate their own codes.

References

Harvey, S., & Goudvis, A. (2007). *Strategies that work: Teaching comprehension for understanding and engagement* (2nd ed.). Portland, ME: Stenhouse.

Tovani, C. (2000). *I read it, but I don't get it: Comprehension strategies for adolescent readers*. Portland, ME: Stenhouse.

Vaughan, J. L., & Estes, T. H. (1986). *Reading and reasoning beyond the primary grades*. Boston, MA: Allyn & Bacon.

Text Codes

Code Symbol	Meaning
*	Very important information; key concept; new information
?	Confusing information; something doesn't make sense; question
!	Wow! Something you find interesting, hard to believe, or unexpected
✓	Something you already knew
V	Something you can visualize; make a picture in your mind
P	You can make a prediction
2 + 2	You put ideas together (synthesize)
X	Something you disagree with or that contradicts what you thought
R	Reminds you of something
T-S	Text-to-Self connection
T-T	Text-to-Text connection
T-W	Text-to-World connection
C	Connects to something you know about
A	Something you agree with

Text Codes

Code Symbol	Meaning
*	Very important information; key concept; new information
?	Confusing information; something doesn't make sense; question
!	Wow! Something you find interesting, hard to believe, or unexpected
✓	Something you already knew
V	Something you can visualize; make a picture in your mind
P	You can make a prediction
2 + 2	You put ideas together (synthesize)
X	Something you disagree with or that contradicts what you thought
R	Reminds you of something
T-S	Text-to-Self connection
T-T	Text-to-Text connection
T-W	Text-to-World connection
C	Connects to something you know about
A	Something you agree with

Discussion Web

Description

The Discussion Web (Alvermann, 1991; Barton, 1995; Duthie, 1986) is a graphic aid for helping students address both sides of an issue. By considering pro and con arguments before drawing a conclusion, active discussion is stimulated. The strategy incorporates reading, speaking, listening, and writing using a think-pair-share approach with students working in cooperative learning groups. Students are encouraged to use their skills in critical thinking and debate when discussing complex issues.

Bridge to the Disciplines

Knowledge in the disciplines is often tentative and challenged. Students' ability to reconcile multiple perspectives on a topic can be scaffolded through the use of a Discussion Web. A Discussion Web supports students' organization of their evidence to support claims when constructing an argument.

Technology Connections

Students can be encouraged to use an online discussion forum to engage in the Discussion Web. Examples include Google Groups, www.chatzy.com, or www.todaysmeet.com. A wiki can be created and group facilitators can post text segments. Group members respond and use the text to support their conclusion. Examples of wikis include www.wikispaces.com or www.pbworks.com.

Text Type
Narrative
Informational

Disciplinary Considerations
- Close reading
- Building prior knowledge
- Mapping graphic representations against explanations in the text
- Posing discipline-relevant questions
- Comparing claims and propositions across texts

Common Core Anchor Standards

Reading
- Read closely to determine what the text says explicitly and to make logical inferences from it; cite specific textual evidence . . . drawn from the text.
- Read and comprehend complex literary and informational texts.

Speaking and Listening
- Prepare for and participate effectively in a range of conversations and collaborations with diverse partners, building on others' ideas and expressing their own clearly and persuasively.

Writing
- Draw evidence from literary or informational texts to support analysis, reflection, and research.

Strategic Behaviors
Inferring
Determining Importance
Synthesizing

Suggested Uses for Disciplinary Literacy
(adapted from Swafford, 1990)

ELA: After reading an essay, students can respond to a question related to the narrator's stance.

History: Names can be substituted for the Yes-No columns and students can use multiple resources to research each person's particular stance related to an issue.

Science: Students might label the columns Hypothesis 1 and Hypothesis 2 and use the columns to support explanations of a scientific question.

Math: After reading a word problem, students can list elements and determine whether they are relevant or not relevant to solving the problem.

Procedure

1. Choose a topic that has the potential to generate opposing viewpoints. Be sure to initially develop an understanding of key vocabulary, survey illustrations and charts, build background knowledge as needed, and help students set purposes for their reading. Then provide the resource materials related to the topic.

2. Display the reproducible on page 14. Duplicate it and distribute copies to students or have them recreate it in their journals. To introduce the Discussion Web, pose a question related to the topic that stimulates opposing views. Have students write the question on their Discussion Web. See sample on page 13.

3. Have students work with a partner or partners to brainstorm at least three responses for each side of the question posed. Encourage students to underline, circle, or write down key words and phrases that may support the responses they have chosen.

4. Have pairs or small groups compare their reasons with another group. Tell the groups that their goal is to work toward consensus. Provide ample time for students to share and discuss what the text materials explicitly state, what inferences can be made, and particular sentences, paragraphs, or text segments that support their conclusions. Encourage students to listen carefully and finally write their conclusion at the bottom of the Web.

5. Provide time for each group to decide which of the group's reasons best support the conclusion they have drawn. Check or star the reasons.

6. Have a spokesperson from each group report to the whole class.

7. If desired, invite students to write their individual conclusions on their Discussion Web, citing specific portions of the text that support their conclusion.

Additional Considerations for Successful Implementation

♦ Encourage students to number the paragraphs, sections, or stanzas of the text selection prior to reading.

♦ At the outset, you may need to post rules for group interaction so that students with opposing viewpoints are listened to and treated with respect during the group discussions.

References

Alvermann, D. (1991). The discussion web: A graphic aid for learning across the curriculum. *The Reading Teacher, 45*, 92–99.

Barton, J. (1995). Conducting effective classroom discussions. *Journal of Reading, 38*, 346–350.

Duthie, J. (1986). The web: A powerful tool for the teaching and evaluation of the expository essay. *The History and Social Studies Teacher, 21*, 232–236.

Swafford, J. (1990, July). *Discussion strategies for improving reading and writing to learn.* Paper presented at the World Congress on Reading, Stockholm, Sweden.

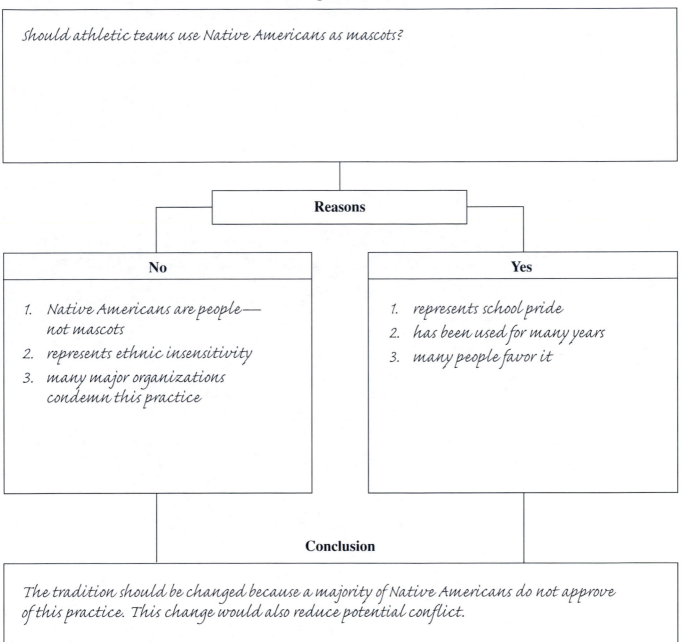

Question

Should athletic teams use Native Americans as mascots?

Reasons

No

1. Native Americans are people—not mascots
2. represents ethnic insensitivity
3. many major organizations condemn this practice

Yes

1. represents school pride
2. has been used for many years
3. many people favor it

Conclusion

The tradition should be changed because a majority of Native Americans do not approve of this practice. This change would also reduce potential conflict.

Discussion Web

Question

Reasons

No	**Yes**

Conclusion

Double-Entry Journal

Description

The Double-Entry Journal (Tovani, 2000, 2011) is a form of guided note taking that helps students track their thinking and interact with text while reading. Similar in format to two-column notes, Double-Entry Journals are more flexible and allow students to respond to their reading and/or listening in a variety of ways. For example, by making connections, noting confusing parts, listing interesting facts or details, drawing a sketch, or noting a difficult vocabulary word, students can respond to their reading and expand their thinking.

Bridge to the Disciplines

Writing Double-Entry Journals helps students to read for information and examine and respond to their content texts from a variety of perspectives. In doing so, they further explore how language is created and communicated in that specific discipline.

Technology Connections

Double-Entry Journals can easily be used in online environments like Google Docs or Evernote (www.evernote. com). Other applications like Voicethread (www.voicethread.com) can be used to upload a Double-Entry Journal and then students can add voice comments about their connections.

Text Type
Narrative
Informational

Disciplinary Considerations
- Building prior knowledge
- Building specialized vocabulary
- Learning to deconstruct complex sentences
- Posing discipline-relevant questions

Common Core Anchor Standards

Reading
- Read closely to determine what the text says explicitly and to make logical inferences from it.
- Delineate and evaluate the argument and specific claims in the text, including the validity of the reasoning as well as the relevance and sufficiency of the evidence.

Writing
- Write routinely over extended time frames . . . and shorter time frames . . . for a range of tasks, purposes, and audiences.

Strategic Behaviors
Monitoring Meaning
Asking Questions
Inferring
Determining Importance
Synthesizing

Suggested Uses for Disciplinary Literacy

ELA: Select quotations from the text and enter them on the left side. On the right side, respond to each quotation, note how it connects to you, or write the insights you gained into a particular character.

History: List major events on the left side and how they are connected or why they are significant.

Science: Is the information presented accurately so that the conclusion drawn is accurate and the experiment could be replicated?

For an experiment, list predictions on the left prior to doing the experiment. Place results on the right, following the experiment.

Math: Is the information presented specific? Are there words that are ambiguous that need clear definition in order to understand the proposition? List the ambiguous words on the left and their meanings, possibly in context, on the right.

Procedure

1. Have students fold a piece of paper in half lengthwise or provide a copy of one of the Double-Entry Journal reproducibles on pages 17–21. An example follows.

Double-Entry Journal for Global Studies

Title _Water: Stuff of Life, Death_

What the Text Says	What I Wonder
1. Bad water—300 million Africans lack access to safe water. Page _1_	1. I wonder what caused the problem?
2. Government doesn't work. Page _3_	2. I wonder what the government of Malawi is like? I wonder why they don't do something?

---

2. Explain to students that on the left side of the paper they will copy sentences, words, or phrases from the text, noting the page(s) on which they were found. On the right side they will track their thinking about the information presented.

3. Introduce the disciplinary strategy for the reading. For example, for critique, a history teacher might say, "As you read, it is important to question the information presented and the arguments supporting it. How much does the author appear to know about this topic? Is the author presenting all sides of the issue? What information is missing?"

4. Read a section of the text aloud. As you read, write down a quotation or phrase from the text. For example, "In our text it says, '300 million Africans lack access to safe water.'" Note that it is discussed on page 1. "On the right side I am going to write, 'I wonder how recent this information is? Africa is a big continent, so which specific areas or countries are being referred to?'"

5. Continue modeling your note taking and What I Wonder questions until you think that students understand how to proceed.

6. Invite students to work individually or in pairs to read the remainder of the selection and create notes and questions using their Double-Entry Journal.

7. When students have completed the reading, invite them to read their quotations and questions and use them as a basis for a class discussion of the reading.

Additional Considerations for Successful Implementation

♦ Start with one response prompt and provide multiple practice opportunities before introducing additional response options.

References

Tovani, C. (2000). *I read it, but I don't get it: Comprehension strategies for adolescent readers*. Portland, ME: Stenhouse.

Tovani, C. (2011). *So what do they really know? Assessment that informs teaching and learning*. Portland, ME: Stenhouse.

Double-Entry Journal

Title _____

What the Text Says	What I Wonder
1. Page _____	1.
2. Page _____	2.
3. Page _____	3.
4. Page _____	4.
5. Page _____	5.
6. Page _____	6.

Double-Entry Journal

Title _____

Information	My Response/Connection
1. Page _____	1.
2. Page _____	2.
3. Page _____	3.
4. Page _____	4.
5. Page _____	5.
6. Page _____	6.

Double-Entry Journal

Title _____

What the Text Says	Why It's Important
1. Page _____	1.
2. Page _____	2.
3. Page _____	3.
4. Page _____	4.
5. Page _____	5.
6. Page _____	6.

Double-Entry Journal

Title _____

I Predict	What Happened
1. Page _____	1.
2. Page _____	2.
3. Page _____	3.
4. Page _____	4.
5. Page _____	5.
6. Page _____	6.

Double-Entry Journal

Title _____

New or Confusing Word	What I Think It Means
1. Page _____	1.
2. Page _____	2.
3. Page _____	3.
4. Page _____	4.
5. Page _____	5.
6. Page _____	6.

Frayer Model

Description

The Frayer Model (Frayer, Fredrick, & Klausmeier, 1969) is a categorization activity that helps students develop a thorough understanding of important concepts. It also provides a visual means of distinguishing items that help define the concept from those that are merely associated with it.

Bridge to the Disciplines

To build disciplinary knowledge, students need to be able to develop conceptual knowledge and use discipline-specific language. The Frayer Model is a scaffold that can help students develop deeper understanding of discipline-specific vocabulary and concepts. The development of discipline-specific vocabulary and concepts is critical to participating in the discourses of the disciplines. The Frayer Model provides an opportunity for students to grapple with disciplinary vocabulary to be used in their discussions and writing.

Technology Connections

The Frayer Model can be used with online whiteboard applications or with a SMART Board. More contextualized examples can also be embedded by students adding links to pictures or videos for examples and non-examples.

Text Type
Narrative
Informational

Disciplinary Considerations
♦ Building prior knowledge
♦ Building specialized vocabulary

Common Core Anchor Standards
Reading
♦ Interpret words and phrases as they are used in a text, including determining technical, connotative, and figurative meanings, and analyze how specific word choices shape meaning or tone.

Strategic Behaviors
Determining Importance
Synthesizing

Suggested Uses for Disciplinary Literacy
ELA: Have students create Frayer Models for literary devices they will use to analyze literature.

History: Have students create Frayer Models for historical concepts.

Science: Have students create Frayer Models for key processes or hierarchical categories.

Math: Have students create Frayer Models for key properties that guide computation.

Procedure

1. Select a key word or concept from the lesson, for example, *ecosystem*.

2. Generate a list of key characteristics of the concept. Key characteristics for *ecosystem* might be *relationships, interactions, surroundings, living things*, and *non-living things*.

3. Introduce the concept to students and show them your list of the key characteristics. Distribute the reproducible on page 25; make copies for the students or have them recreate in their notebooks. In small cooperative groups, have students generate examples of the concept. Record responses on the Frayer Model graphic organizer. Examples of ecosystems might be *forests, cities, deserts*, and *oceans*.

4. Have students read the selection and check to see if the characteristics and examples are accurate. Take time to clarify the meaning for nonessential characteristics and non-examples.

5. Have students add nonessential characteristics and non-examples of the concept to their organizer. Some items from their original list of characteristics and examples may need to be moved to other sections of the model based on their reading and collaborating with their peers. Depending on the specific ecosystem under consideration, nonessential characteristics of an ecosystem might be *glaciers, insects, buildings,* or *birds.* Non-examples of an ecosystem might be *automobiles, solutions,* or *electricity.*

6. Once students are secure in the essential and nonessential characteristics as well as examples and non-examples of the concept, have them relate the concept to a subordinate concept, a superordinate concept, and finally, a coordinate term. For example, a subordinate concept for ecosystem might be *habitat.* A super-ordinate concept might be *environment.* A similar or coordinate phrase might be *community of organisms.*

7. Once students have a conceptual understanding of the term, they should be encouraged to use the term in subsequent discussions and writing when appropriate.

Additional Considerations for Successful Implementation

♦ After students have multiple opportunities to practice, begin to have students self-select conceptual vocabulary.

Reference

Frayer, D. A., Fredrick, W. C., & Klausmeier, H. J. (1969). *A schema for testing the level of concept mastery: Report from the project on situational variables and efficiency of concept learning.* Madison, WI: Wisconsin Research and Development Center for Cognitive Learning.

Sample Frayer Model for **Biology**

Essential Characteristics	Nonessential Characteristics
Have organized nuclei	Contain chlorophyll
Flagella or cilia	Sexual
Unicellular	Asexual
Microscopic	Capture food
Live in water or damp places	

PROTIST

Examples	Nonexamples
Euglena	Animals
Diatoms	Fungi
Protozoa	Plants
Slime molds	Monerans
Paramecia	

A word that means about the same as protist is ___*protista*___.

A word that is more general than protist is ___*organism*___.

A word that is more specific than protist is ___*protozoa*___.

Sample Frayer Model for **Math**

Essential Characteristics	Nonessential Characteristics
Natural elements, their opposites, and zero	The "+" sign
Is a number	May be positive
Has no fraction part	May be negative
Has no decimal part	May be zero

INTEGER

Examples	Nonexamples
5	$\frac{-15}{2}$
100	
−73	1.25
2	0.5
0	$\sqrt{2}$
325	

A word that means about the same as integer is ___*signed number*___.

A word that is more general than integer is ___*rational number*___.

A word that is more specific than integer is ___*whole number*___.

Frayer Model

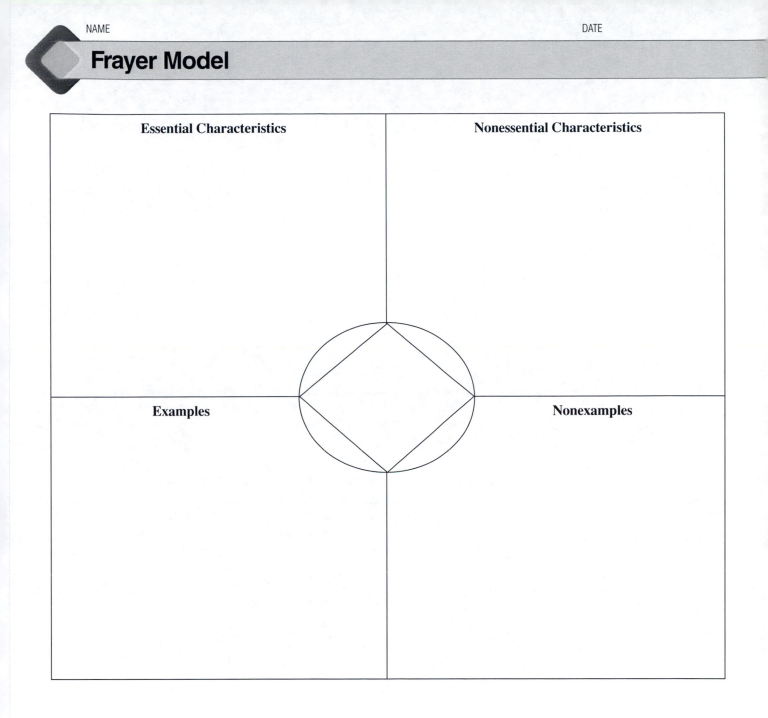

Essential Characteristics	**Nonessential Characteristics**
Examples	**Nonexamples**

A word that means about the same as the key term is _____.

A word that is more general than the key term is _____.

A word that is more specific than the key term is _____.

GIST

Description

GIST (Cunningham, 1982, 2013) is a strategy that provides a structure for students' summary writing. GIST facilitates construction of a complete summary of a text. It is completed during the reading of a text passage. Students chunk texts into smaller parts and construct an accumulating summary that builds after each chunk of text is read.

Bridge to the Disciplines

In order for students to be able to critique a text in a discipline, they first need to come to an overarching understanding of the text. GIST is a scaffold that helps students construct a sense of the main message of the text so that they can interrogate the text further for more disciplinary purposes or build background knowledge necessary for the reading of other texts.

Technology Connections

GIST summaries can be tweeted (www.twitter.com) or posted on a collaborative notes platform like Padlet (www.padlet.com) that limit the user to 140 characters.

Text Type

Narrative
Informational

Disciplinary Considerations

- Close reading
- Building prior knowledge
- Using knowledge of text structures and genres to predict main and subordinate ideas

Common Core Anchor Standards

Reading

- Determine central ideas or themes of a text and analyze their development; summarize the key supporting details and ideas.

Writing

- Write informative/explanatory texts to examine and convey complex ideas and information clearly and accurately through the effective selection, organization, and analysis of content.

Strategic Behaviors

Determining Importance
Summarizing

Suggested Uses for Disciplinary Literacy

ELA: Have students write a GIST summary of a piece of literary non-fiction to later be used in the analysis of fiction.

History: Have students write a GIST summary of a secondary source in order to use that background knowledge to evaluate a primary source on the same topic.

Science: Have students summarize a passage of text that describes a scientific process in order to use that knowledge to construct a scientific model of that process.

Math: Have students write a GIST summary of a text explanation of how to solve a problem. Students can then use that summary to guide their written explanation of how they came to their answer.

Procedure

1. Duplicate the GIST reproducible on page 28 or have students create their own GIST template.

2. Select a passage of text that is one to two pages long. The text should be one that is challenging.

3. Ask students to chunk the text into three to five smaller passages. Examples may be by paragraphs or text headings. If you are introducing the strategy for the first time, model the process by thinking aloud about your process for chunking the text.

4. Read aloud the first chunked passage and model an initial 20-word summary about the first chunk of text.

5. Have students read the second chunked passage and write a second 20-word summary about both chunks of text. Students can complete the second summary in pairs. Project multiple student examples of the second summary.

6. Students read the third chunked passage of text and independently write a 20-word or less summary about all three chunks of text.

Sample GIST for **Math**

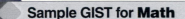

1st Passage

Numerical expressions must have one value which can be found using order of operations.

2nd Passage

To find a value start with 1) evaluating expressions inside parentheses, 2) evaluating all powers, 3) multiplication/division, 4) additions/subtraction

3rd Passage

Algebraic expressions contain unknown variables. To find the unknown substitute values and follow the order of operations.

7. The process continues until students read the entire passage and have written a 20-word or less summary about the entire passage.

8. After students have completed their summaries, have students share in small groups to compare how they summarized the entire text.

Additional Considerations for Successful Implementation

- Fade the scaffold of chunking the text for students and have them chunk the texts independently.
- Have students orally read the text chunks in pairs.

References

Cunningham, J. W. (1982). Generating interactions between schemata and text. In J. Niles & L. Harris (Eds.), *New inquiries in reading research and instruction: Thirty-first yearbook of the National Reading Conference* (pp. 42–47). Washington, DC: National Reading Conference.

Cunningham, J. W. (2013). Research on text complexity: The Common Core State Standards as catalyst. In S. B. Neuman & L. B. Gambrell (Eds.), *Quality reading instruction in the age of Common Core Standards* (pp. 136–148). Newark, DE: International Reading Association.

GIST

1st Passage

_____

_____

_____

2nd Passage

_____

_____

_____

3rd Passage

_____

_____

_____

4th Passage

_____

_____

_____

Final Summary

_____

_____

_____

I-Chart

Description

The Inquiry Chart or I-Chart (Assaf, Ash, Saunders, & Johnson, 2011; Hoffman, 1992) is an organizational scaffold for synthesizing across multiple texts to address a larger inquiry question. It is an organizational tool for developing sub-questions related to an overall inquiry question. Students can also add their own prior knowledge and generate additional questions using the I-Chart.

Bridge to the Disciplines

Inquiry is a critical element in disciplinary literacy. Inquiry can be guided or less structured. The I-Chart provides a guided structure for student inquiry. This scaffold is best used as a way to organize large amounts of information on a topic or in response to an inquiry question. The I-Chart can also be used for a larger task like an essay, digital story, or presentation.

Technology Connections

The I-Chart is ideal for Internet research when students encounter multiple texts. The chart can also be used electronically as a Google Form or Google Doc.

Text Type
Narrative
Informational

Disciplinary Considerations
- Posing discipline-relevant questions
- Comparing claims and propositions across texts
- Using norms for reasoning within the discipline (i.e., what counts as evidence to evaluate claims)

Common Core Anchor Standards
Reading
- Integrate and evaluate content presented in diverse media and formats, including visually and quantitatively, as well as in words.

Writing
- Conduct short as well as more sustained research projects based on focused questions, demonstrating understanding of the subject under investigation.

Strategic Behaviors
Determining Importance
Synthesizing

Suggested Uses for Disciplinary Literacy
ELA: Use as a scaffold for an I-Search paper or research paper.

History: Use with a document-based question (DBQ) or historical research.

Science: Use as a scaffold for an investigation or experiment.

Math: Use to investigate a theorem by reading multiple examples.

Procedure

1. Select an overarching question to investigate related to a topic or area your class is studying. Examples might include, "Should the United States have dropped the atomic bomb?" or "What causes cell division?" You can have students brainstorm potential inquiry questions in small groups.

2. Provide multiple sources for students on the topic or have students search and locate sources for their topic using the Internet and library research.

3. Distribute the I-Chart reproducible on page 31. You can provide students with a predetermined set of sub-questions or have students generate their own sub-questions.

4. Model an example of a sub-question and how a source addresses one or more of the sub-questions. See the example on page 30.

Sample I-Chart for **Social Studies**

Inquiry Question: Should criminal penalties be placed on people who sell or rent violent video games to a minor? (from www.deliberating.org)

	Question 1 Are video games violent?	**Question 2** Do video games cause violence?	**Question 3** Are minors targeted for violent video game sales?	**Other Important Evidence**	**New Questions**
What I Already Know	The games I play are violent.	I play video games and I am not violent.	I have to have my parents buy some games for me.		What laws protect minors from buying violent games?
Source 1 Deliberating in a democracy	Study from Kent State University found video game violence disturbingly high.	There is "less data" on the effects.	80% of sales are violent games. 50% of youth favor violent games.		
Source 2 NPR Article: "Video game release suspended"	Grand Theft Auto is considered violent. There are several acts of violence in the game.	No evidence is provided.	Grand Theft Auto did receive an adult rating.		

5. Individually, in pairs, or in small groups, students should create additional sub-questions to help address their larger inquiry question.

6. Model the process for selecting the relevant details to include in your response.

7. Students then write the key ideas and details from each text that address each of the sub-questions. Students can complete individually or in pairs.

8. Have students share their responses by projecting on the board. Ask students to support their responses by directing their peers back to specific text passages.

9. After reading multiple sources, students should then write a summary response for each sub-question based on all of the texts read.

Additional Considerations for Successful Implementation

♦ Initially you can provide the sub-questions on the chart. See the reproducible on page 31. See sample above.

♦ If the question is more binary in nature, like "Should the United States have dropped the atomic bomb?", you can have students first evaluate whether the text supports, refutes, or is unclear in addressing the sub-questions by adding Yes, No, and Maybe for students to circle (see the reproducible on page 32).

References

Assaf, L., Ash, G., Saunders, J., & Johnson, J. (2011). Renewing two seminal literacy practices: I-Charts and I-Search papers. *English Journal, 18*(4), 31–42.

Hoffman, J. (1992). Critical reading/thinking across the curriculum: Using I-Charts to support learning. *Language Arts, 69*(2), 121–127.

I-Chart

Inquiry Question:

	Question 1	Question 2	Question 3	Other Important Evidence	New Questions
What I Already Know					
Source 1					
Source 2					
Source 3					
Summary					

I-Chart

Inquiry Question:

Text Source	Sub Question			Sub Question			Sub Question		
	Yes	No	Maybe	Yes	No	Maybe	Yes	No	Maybe
	Yes	No	Maybe	Yes	No	Maybe	Yes	No	Maybe
	Yes	No	Maybe	Yes	No	Maybe	Yes	No	Maybe
	Yes	No	Maybe	Yes	No	Maybe	Yes	No	Maybe
Your Opinion	Yes	No	Maybe	Yes	No	Maybe	Yes	No	Maybe

Informational Text Structures

Description

Understanding how a text is organized can help students better grasp the ideas within it. Graphic organizers can be a powerful learning tool to help students learn the five major types of informational text organization. Graphic organizers can also serve as a framework for recording notes that can be used for review and study.

Bridge to the Disciplines

Disciplinary texts can make use of a variety of text structures. Using graphic organizers designed to highlight the various types of Informational Text Structures helps students to read and understand how key ideas are presented in a text. In doing so, they further explore, in a visual way, how language is structured in that particular discipline.

Technology Connections

There are several online platforms for constructing graphic organizers, such as www.bubbl.us, www.mindomo.com, or www.dabbleboard.com. Applications for the iPad that can be used to create graphic organizers include Skitch, Explain Everything, or ShowMe.

Text Type
Informational

Disciplinary Considerations

- Build prior knowledge
- Use knowledge of text structures and genres to predict main ideas and subordinate details
- Mapping graphic (and mathematical) representations against explanations in the text

Common Core Anchor Standards
Reading

- Read closely to determine what the text says explicitly.
- Analyze the structure of texts.
- Integrate and evaluate content presented in diverse media and formats, including visually and quantitatively, as well as in words.

Strategic Behaviors

Using Prior Knowledge
Asking Questions
Inferring
Determining Importance
Synthesizing

Suggested Uses for Disciplinary Literacy

ELA: Have students use an informational text structure to identify the argument presented in a piece of literary non-fiction.

History: After an introduction to types of text features, have students preview their text materials, seeking and identifying those features.

Science: Tables and graphs are integral parts of most science materials. Have students peruse the text materials typical in the class and note pages and topics of each table and/or graph. Discuss the importance of using the information they present in understanding the major ideas in the text.

Math: Have students survey their textbook to identify how chapters and sections are organized and to find resources that will be helpful to use in each chapter.

Procedure

1. A succinct overview of the five major types of Informational Text Structures is found on page 35. Review the five structures and select one that represents a typical text in your discipline. Examples showing how the five text structures are used in history are found on page 36.

2. Tell students that graphic organizers are useful tools to help them understand how the information in a text is organized so that they can better understand and remember it.

3. Show one graphic organizer and model how to complete it. For example, you might say something like the following if the compare/contrast example on page 42 is used: "Look at the brief passage about the English language that I have given you and follow along as I read it. [Read the passage aloud.] Look at the text pattern I am showing you. You can see that it is comparison and contrast. There is no title, so I won't fill that in, but who or what is being compared? [Invite a student to respond.] That's correct. It is comparing two versions of the English language. I'll write the phrase here on the organizer. Now let's see if we can list some ways the two variations of English are alike and different." Guide students as needed and complete the organizer.

4. Provide copies of the reproducible on page 42 for students. Then assign an example from your content area that is of the same type of text structure that you modeled. If your students have access to technology, you might say, "Use the hyperlink the author has put in your textbook and your personal technology device to read and complete the organizer, looking for ways ideas are being compared (how they are alike) and contrasted (how they differ)." You may initially want students to work with partners or in small groups to complete the organizer.

5. Give students ample opportunity to complete the organizer, and then invite sharing between individuals or small groups and then with the whole class. Clarify misunderstandings and expand student responses as needed.

6. Systematically introduce other graphic organizers using a similar procedure. Be sure to help students understand how graphic organizers can be keys to understanding how an author presents ideas and what the key ideas are. Point out how the completed organizers can be useful for review and study. See pages 37–45 for reproducibles exemplifying different text structures.

7. As students become more familiar with graphic organizers, you may want to introduce the signal words listed on pages 35 and 46 that are often clues to particular text types. These clues can often help students determine the organization of a text.

8. Once the text structures most frequently used in your content area have been taught, you may want to enlarge or adapt the chart on page 35 as a concise summary that can be a part of a bulletin board or a review sheet for students to scan and place in your class file in their personal technology devices.

Informational Text Structures

Text Pattern	Description	Signal Words	Graphic Organizer
Main Idea/Supporting Details (Description)	Key concept or idea and details about characteristics, attributes, features, actions, examples	For instance, for example, to begin with, that is, also, such as, in fact, along with, in addition to, in other words, as, specifically, furthermore, most important	
Time Order/Sequence	Information is given in chronological or numerical order	First, second, third, on (date), at, not long after, now, during, next, then, last, later, when, before, earlier	
Compare/Contrast	How two or more things are alike and/or different	However, on the other hand, but, yet, as well as, like/unlike, in contrast, similarly, on the contrary, likewise, although, instead, otherwise, while, rather, most, same, as opposed to	
Cause/Effect	Ideas, events, or facts are presented with effects or facts that happen as a result	Because, if/then, since, therefore, consequently, as a result, nevertheless, thus, subsequently, so, for this reason, due to, this led to, so that	
Problem/Solution	A problem is stated with one or more solutions offered	Problem is, question is, dilemma is, if/then, because, so that, question/answer, conclude, a solution is, propose that	

Main Idea/Supporting Details (Description)

A key concept or idea is presented followed by more information about the concept or idea.

Example

Main Idea   The monarchs themselves were regularly in France.

Supporting Details   William I spent half his reign in Normandy. William II and Henry I also spent half of their reigns there, as did Henry II, who lived there for as many as twenty years.

Time Order/Sequence

Information is given in the order that it happened or in a sequence.

Example

By the thirteenth century, English was the dominant language in the Lowland south and east. By 1400 the Scottish dialect had evolved. By the 1500s, it was clear that a standard dialect was emerging throughout the land.

Compare/Contrast

Information shows how two or more things are alike and/or different.

Example

Two variations of the English language emerged, Middle English and Standard English. Both were used throughout the land, but different regions began to use one or the other predominantly.

In Middle English, all dialects were equal and written language contained a wide range of forms, each being acceptable. No one minded if a writer spelled a word differently in different parts of the same text.

With the rise of Standard English, agreement arose about how things should be said and written. As more people became able to read and write, the need for norms grew. There was a growing sense of shared usage.

Cause/Effect

Ideas, events, or facts are presented with things that happen as a result.

Example

As more people became able to read and write, the need for a standardized language became apparent.

Problem/Solution

A problem is given and one or more solutions are offered.

Example

In the 1500s, there was a huge amount of variation in how language was used and written. As more people learned to read and write, the variation in language usage hindered communication. In order to solve the problem, people needed to work together to develop a common style. Many people needed to interact regularly and frequently.

Compare and Contrast Text Pattern

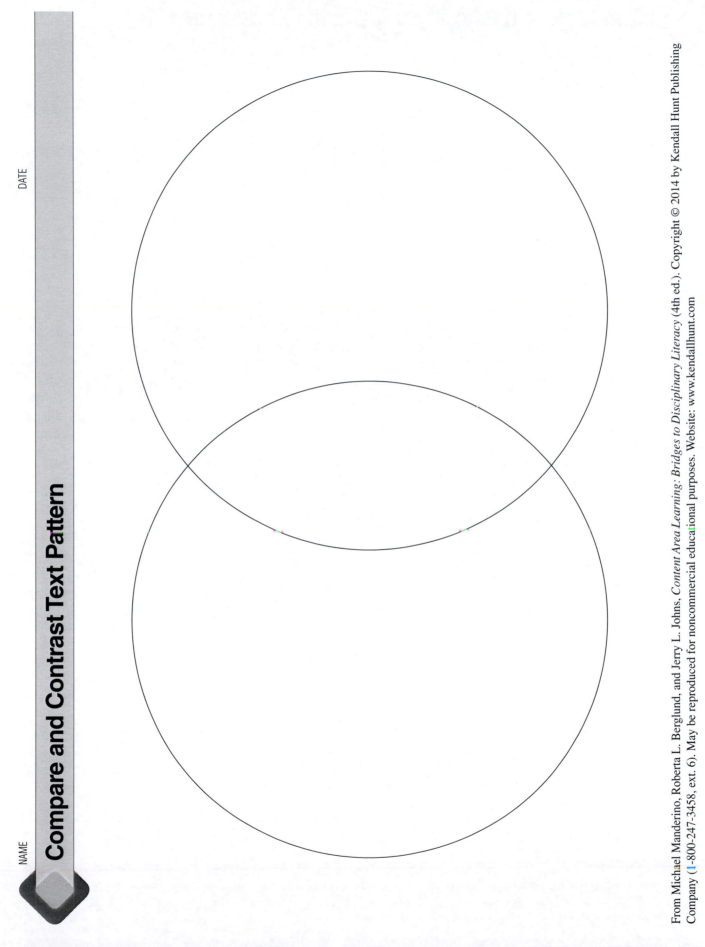

From Michael Manderino, Roberta L. Berglund, and Jerry L. Johns, *Content Area Learning: Bridges to Disciplinary Literacy* (4th ed.). Copyright © 2014 by Kendall Hunt Publishing Company (1-800-247-3458, ext. 6). May be reproduced for noncommercial educational purposes. Website: www.kendallhunt.com

Main Idea and Supporting Details Text Pattern

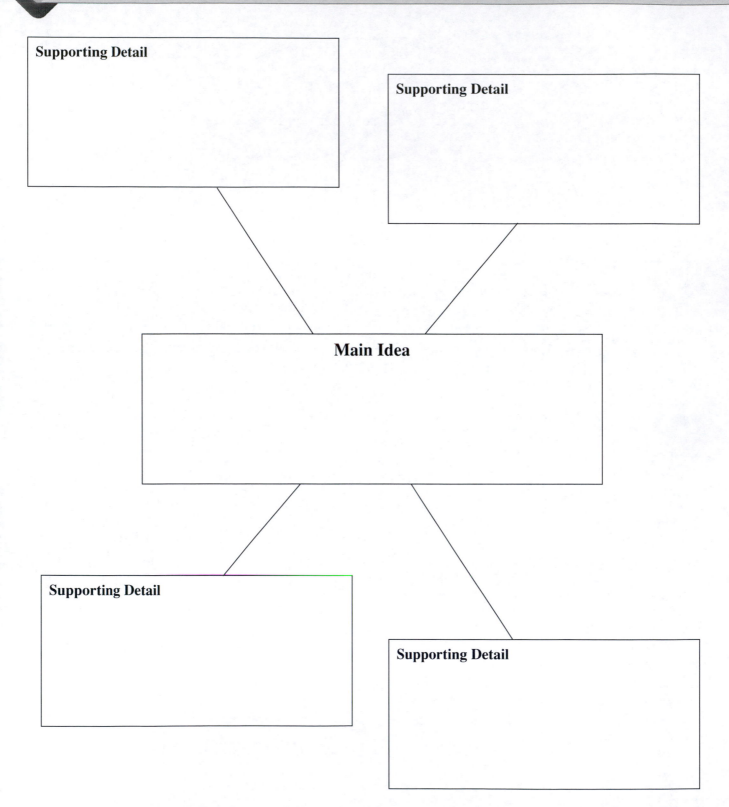

Supporting Detail

Supporting Detail

Main Idea

Supporting Detail

Supporting Detail

Main Idea and Supporting Details Text Pattern

Main Idea

Supporting Details

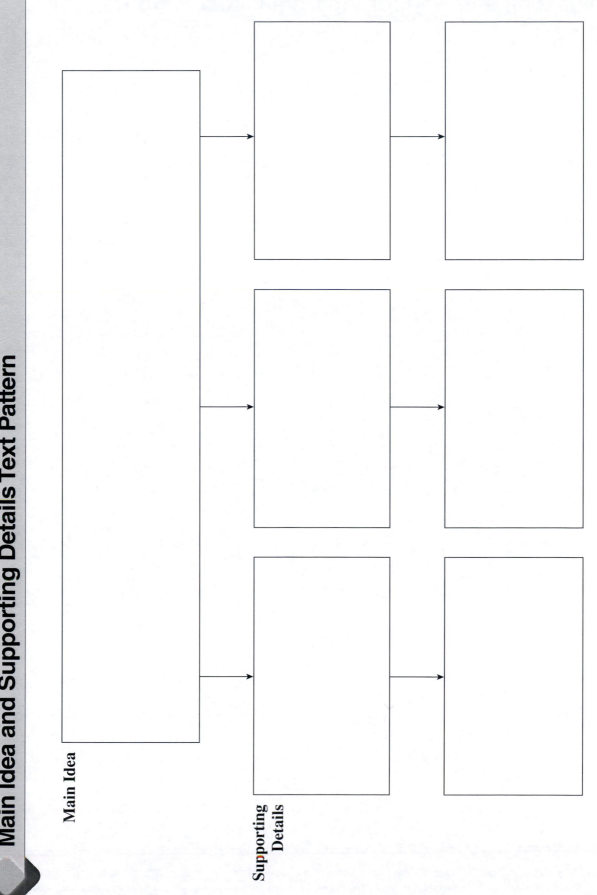

From Michael Manderino, Roberta L. Berglund, Jerry L. Johns, *Content Area Learning: Bridges to Disciplinary Literacy* (4th ed). Copyright © 2014 by Kendall Hunt Publishing Company (1-800-247-3458, ext. 6). May be reproduced for noncommercial educational purposes. Website: www.kendallhunt.com

Main Idea and Supporting Details Text Pattern

Main Idea

Sequence of Events Text Pattern

```
┌─────────────────────────────────────────────────────────┐
│                                                         │
│                                                         │
└─────────────────────────────────────────────────────────┘
                            │
                            ▼
┌─────────────────────────────────────────────────────────┐
│                                                         │
│                                                         │
└─────────────────────────────────────────────────────────┘
                            │
                            ▼
┌─────────────────────────────────────────────────────────┐
│                                                         │
│                                                         │
└─────────────────────────────────────────────────────────┘
                            │
                            ▼
┌─────────────────────────────────────────────────────────┐
│                                                         │
│                                                         │
└─────────────────────────────────────────────────────────┘
                            │
                            ▼
┌─────────────────────────────────────────────────────────┐
│                                                         │
│                                                         │
└─────────────────────────────────────────────────────────┘
                            │
                            ▼
┌─────────────────────────────────────────────────────────┐
│                                                         │
│                                                         │
└─────────────────────────────────────────────────────────┘
                            │
                            ▼
┌─────────────────────────────────────────────────────────┐
│                                                         │
│                                                         │
└─────────────────────────────────────────────────────────┘
```

Compare and Contrast Text Pattern

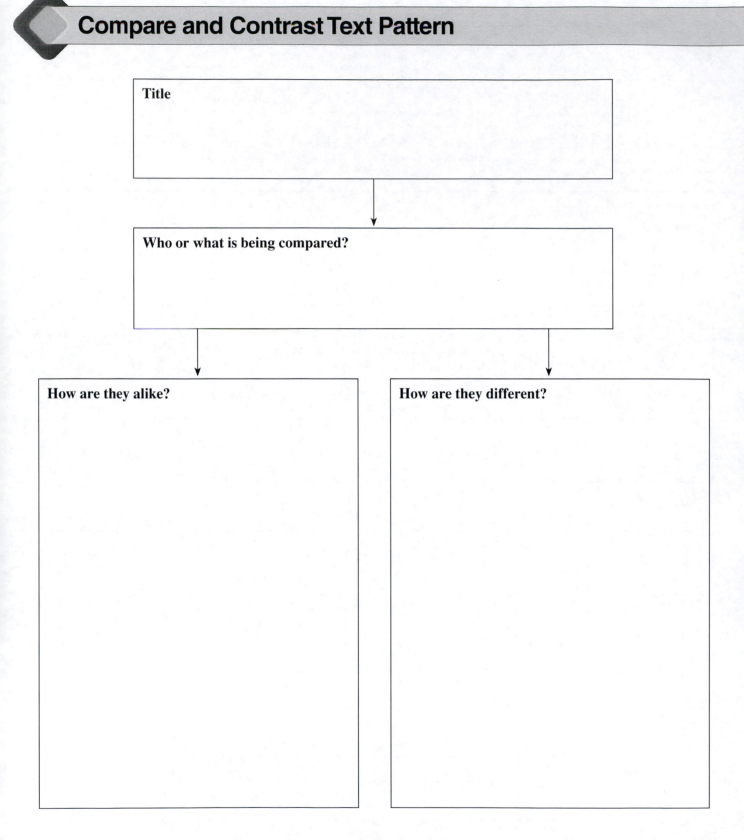

Title

Who or what is being compared?

How are they alike?

How are they different?

Cause and Effect Text Pattern

CAUSE

EFFECT

Why Something Happens

What Happens

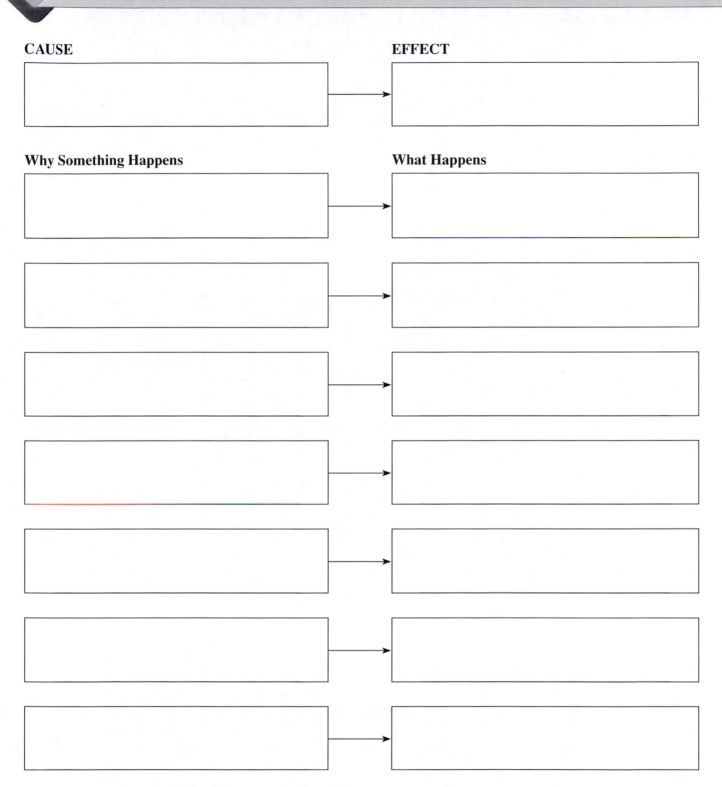

Cause and Effect Text Pattern: Chain of Related Events

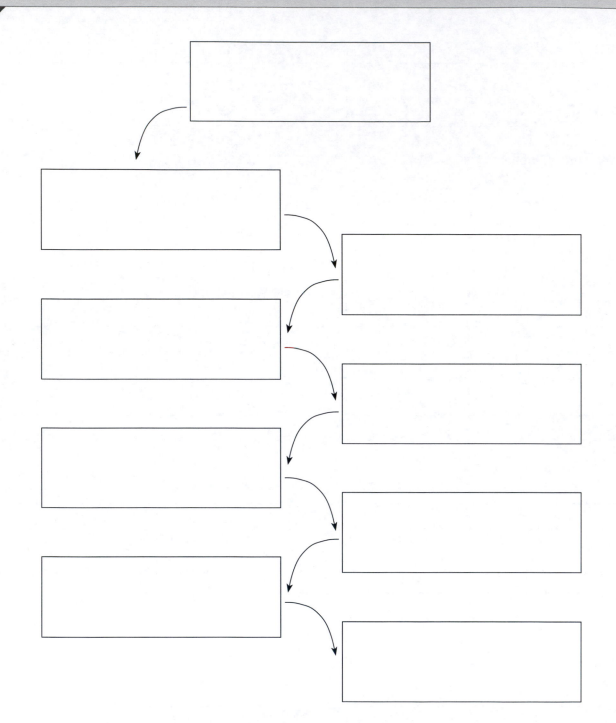

Problem and Solution Text Pattern

Problem

Attempts

Outcomes

Solution

Signal Words (Clues to Text Types)

Main Idea/Details (Description)

For instance	Also	In addition to	Specifically
For example	Such as	In other words	Furthermore
To begin with	In fact	As	Most important
That is	Along with		

Time Order/Sequence

First	At	Next	When
Second	Not long after	Then	Before
Third	Now	Last	Earlier
On (date)	During	Later	

Compare/Contrast

However	Like/unlike	Although	Rather
On the other hand	In contrast	Instead	Most
But	Similarly	Otherwise	Same
Yet	On the contrary	While	As opposed to
As well as	Likewise		

Cause/Effect

Because	Consequently	Subsequently	Due to
If/then	As a result	So	This led to
Since	Nevertheless	For this reason	So that
Therefore	Thus		

Problem/Solution

Problem is	If/then	Question/answer	A solution is
Question is	Because	Conclude	Propose that
Dilemma is	So that		

Intra-Act

Description

The Intra-Act strategy (Hoffman, 1979) encourages students to construct their own decisions about issues by making intertextual links. In four steps, students move from formulating opinions based solely upon one text to ultimately basing their opinions upon further research, group discussions, and reflection. The four steps are: 1) students construct meaning from a text selection; 2) students make connections between the information in the first text and other resources they find on the topic; 3) students share their own reactions on the topic and the insights or values those reactions convey; and 4) students reflect on those newly formed insights or values.

Bridge to the Disciplines

Knowledge in the disciplines can be tentative and challenged. Students' ability to reconcile multiple perspectives on the topic can be scaffolded through the use of the Intra-Act strategy. Intra-Act provides opportunities for students to verbally interact with their peers in order to construct disciplinary understandings of a topic.

Technology Connections

Students can record their responses using a collaborative Google document or using Evernote. They could also use iPads and the Internet for researching and accessing multiple texts on the topic.

Text Type
Narrative
Informational

Disciplinary Considerations
♦ Comparing claims and propositions across texts
♦ Using norms for reasoning within the discipline (i.e., what counts as evidence) to evaluate claims

Common Core Anchor Standards
Reading
♦ Integrate and evaluate content presented in diverse media and formats, including visually and quantitatively, as well as in words.
♦ Analyze how two or more texts address similar themes or topics in order to build knowledge or to compare the approaches the authors take.

Speaking and Listening
♦ Evaluate a speaker's point of view, reasoning, and use of evidence and rhetoric.

Strategic Behaviors
Using Prior Knowledge
Asking Questions
Inferring
Synthesizing

Suggested Uses for Disciplinary Literacy

ELA: Have students read multiple interpretations of a work of literature and use Intra-Act to support student generation of their own text-supported inferences and conclusions.

History: Have students read competing accounts of a controversial historical event and use Intra-Act to scaffold students' development of their interpretation of the event.

Science: Have students read multiple sources related to a scientific phenomenon and use Intra-Act to support students' causal explanations of that phenomenon.

Math: Have students read multiple approaches to solving a problem and use Intra-Act to support students' decisions for how to best solve a particular problem type.

Procedure

1. Explain to students the difference between topics that are explanatory, such as how a bill becomes a law, and topics that are subject to opinion, such as whether certain bills should become laws.

2. Use the sample topic and chart that follows or develop an example from your curriculum to model how the Intra-Act strategy works. Show examples of statements to the students. Brainstorm with students other statements that could be made to stimulate debate and discussion on the sample topic.

Sample of Intra-Act for Social Studies

Topic _Was it appropriate for the United States to enter into the Iraq War?_

(Write group members' names, including your own, in the top row of blanks.)

Statements	José	Anna	Tom	Xiao Peng
The U.S. has an obligation to enforce justice and world peace.	yes	no	yes	yes
We had no business being across the world in someone else's fight.	yes	yes	no	no
We (the U.S.) were the best candidates to eliminate Saddam Hussein.	no	no	yes	no
We should have spent all the money that was spent on the Iraq War on our public schools instead.	yes	no	yes	no

3. Either on your own or with students' input, choose another controversial topic for which you can locate several sources. The topic should be one that lends itself to differing opinions.

4. Assign the first reading on the controversial topic. Following the reading, brainstorm with students possible claim statements that can be made about the reading. It should be possible to answer the statements with either yes or no. Choose four of the statements and write them under *Statements* on the reproducible or in their own student-created Intra-Act charts.

5. Assign students to work in small heterogeneous groups (three to four students per group). The groups should take seven to ten minutes to summarize and discuss the reading. Assign a leader in each group to share and report the summary of the reading.

6. Allow students class time to research their topics using other printed and media sources. You may wish to enlist the help of your school's librarian or media specialist to provide a wide variety of relevant material for your classroom. Instruct students to be prepared to share and discuss their findings in their next group meeting.

7. Schedule time for students to meet in their small groups to compare their research findings and any conclusions they have about the topic.

8. After students have explored the topic more thoroughly, they will begin the evaluative phase of the discussion. In this phase, students work independently. First, students fill in the names of each of their group members across the top row of the grid. Next, they write yes or no under their own name in response to each statement. Finally, they predict how each member of their group will respond to the statements and write yes or no under each member's name after each statement.

9. Students meet again with their groups and share their response statements. As each student shares, group members should record the evidence used by their peers in each corresponding box and compare the students' responses to their predictions.

10. Finally, open the discussion to the whole class. Encourage students to share the reasons for their responses and allow opportunities to challenge, support, and question one another. Students should use text evidence to support their responses. This is an opportune time to reinforce student skills of offering constructive criticism and disagreeing respectfully and assertively, not aggressively.

Additional Considerations for Successful Implementation

♦ Teachers can provide more of the sources with initial attempts at this type of inquiry.

♦ Additional discussions about searching, locating, and evaluating additional resources, including Internet sites, may be necessary.

© William Perugini, 2014. Under license from Shutterstock, Inc.

Reference

Hoffman, J. V. (1979). The Intra-Act procedure for critical reading. *Journal of Reading, 22*, 605–608.

Intra-Act

Topic _____

(Write group members' names, including your own, in the top row of blanks.)

Statements				

Directions

1. Think about the above statements and then under your name write *yes* if you agree with the statement or *no* if you disagree with the statement.

2. Under each member's name, predict how that person will respond to the statements by writing *yes* or *no* by each statement under the name.

3. When you meet with your group, compare your predictions to how members really answered.

4. When the class meets to discuss the statements, use the information you found in your research to help you challenge, support, or question your own and others' opinions. Remember to listen well, support your responses with your research, and be respectful to others in your responses.

Knowledge Rating

Description

Knowledge Rating (Beck, McKeown, & Kucan, 2013; Blachowicz, 1986; Blachowicz & Fisher, 2014) is a prereading activity that encourages students to develop sensitivity to and awareness of words by responding to a list of words that reflects the content of an upcoming lesson. This self-evaluation strategy serves to activate prior knowledge and helps students to make predictions about what is to be learned. Because what students already know about the content is one of the strongest indicators of how well they will learn new information about it (Marzano, 2004), using a Knowledge Rating chart prior to instruction can also help to assess students' readiness for instruction. Using the Knowledge Rating chart and participating in related discussion also helps students understand that word meanings evolve over time with use and experience.

Bridge to the Disciplines

Disciplinary vocabulary is often used in very technical ways that may contradict more general meanings. For example, the word *mean* used in math has a specific meaning as opposed to the ways students may use it to describe behavior. Completing a Knowledge Rating chart helps students become familiar with the critical vocabulary and the ways it is specifically used in the discipline. It also provides insights into what information is valued in that discipline.

Technology Connections

Knowledge Rating charts can be used collaboratively by creating the chart using Google Docs or a Google spreadsheet.

Text Type
Narrative
Informational

Disciplinary Considerations
◆ Building prior knowledge
◆ Building specialized vocabulary
◆ Posing discipline-relevant questions

Common Core Anchor Standards
Language
◆ Determine or clarify the meaning of unknown and multiple-meaning words.
◆ Acquire and use accurately a range of general academic and domain-specific words.

Strategic Behaviors
Using Prior Knowledge
Asking Questions

Suggested Uses for Disciplinary Literacy
ELA: Use Knowledge Rating before, during, and after reading a novel or selection, connecting the essential themes with issues in today's world.

History: Use Knowledge Rating to assess student knowledge of causes and effects of historical events.

Science: Use Knowledge Rating before, during, and after reading the text and online resources.

Math: Use Knowledge Rating to determine student understanding of mathematical functions.

Procedure

1. Select several vocabulary words that are important to the concepts in the lesson.

2. Write these words on the Knowledge Rating reproducible on page 53. Duplicate and distribute it to students or send it to students electronically. An example follows.

Sample Knowledge Rating for **Literature**

Directions: Below are some words that you will find in your lesson. Rate your knowledge for each of the words by placing an X under the category you have chosen.

Adventures of Huckleberry Finn

Word	(1) Know It Well, Can Explain It and Use It	(2) Think I Know Something About It	(3) Have Heard/Seen It, but Don't Know What It Means	(4) Do Not Know the Word
1. *dismal*	X			
2. *widow*	X			
3. *stretchers*			X	

3. Invite students to rate their knowledge of each word according to the categories you have chosen. For the purpose of the example, you may want to use these categories: 1) Know It Well, Can Explain It and Use It; 2) Think I Know Something About It; 3) Have Heard/Seen It, but Don't Know What It Means; and 4) Do Not Know the Word.

4. When students have completed their rating, divide the class into small groups and have them discuss their knowledge of each word. Invite students to define those words that fall into the Know It Well category.

5. Circulate through the classroom while students are discussing the words. Listen to their comments to determine their knowledge of or misconceptions about the words.

6. Conduct a brief discussion with the whole group. Invite students to make predictions about the content of the lesson based on their enhanced knowledge of some of the words on the chart. You might also generate a list of questions that students hope to be able to answer through the lesson.

7. As students participate in the lesson, highlight words as they are encountered. Have students decide if their predictions for the words were correct regarding their meaning.

Additional Considerations for Successful Implementation

♦ Provide a column for students to write the meaning of each word after they have completed the lesson.

♦ Use these headings on the Knowledge Rating: 1) I know this so well I could teach it to someone else; 2) I understand this, but can't quite explain it; and 3) I really don't get this yet.

♦ Provide a list of words and have students rate them from 1–4 with 1 being "I don't know it at all" and 4 being "I know it well and could teach it to someone else."

♦ Have students write the meaning of words before instruction in one column and the correct meaning after instruction and discussion in another column.

References

Beck, I. L., McKeown, M. G., & Kucan, L. (2013). *Bringing words to life: Robust vocabulary instruction* (2nd ed.). New York, NY: Guilford.

Blachowicz, C. L. Z. (1986). Making connections: Alternatives to the vocabulary notebook. *Journal of Reading, 29*, 643–649.

Blachowicz, C., & Fisher, P. J. (2014). *Teaching vocabulary in all classrooms* (5th ed.). Upper Saddle River, NJ: Pearson.

Marzano, R. J. (2004). *Building background knowledge for academic achievement: Research on what works in schools*. Alexandria, VA: Association for Supervision and Curriculum Development.

Knowledge Rating

Directions: Below are some words that you will find in your lesson. Rate your knowledge for each of the words by placing an X under the category you have chosen.

Title _____

Word	(1) Know It Well, Can Explain It and Use It	(2) Think I Know Something About It	(3) Have Heard/Seen It, but Don't Know What It Means	(4) Do Not Know the Word

List-Group-Label

Description

List-Group-Label, also known as Semantic Mapping when graphically represented (Heimlich & Pittelman, 1986; Johnson & Pearson, 1984; Pearson & Johnson, 1978; Taba, 1967), helps students to organize information in categorical form. By classifying and categorizing information, students become active readers and, in the process, remember new vocabulary and information.

Bridge to the Disciplines

Classifying and categorizing information is an important step to be able to critique and build on that existing body of knowledge. For example, in science it is important to be able to classify and categorize properties of solids, liquids, and gasses. The classification of these properties provides a framework for further analysis of different examples of solids, liquids, and gasses. In history, categorizing causes along social, political, and economic dimensions is important to be able to make claims about, and interpretations of, an historical event.

Technology Connections

Categorization activities like List-Group-Label can be used on a SMART Board where key terms can be moved around. Web-based platforms like Padlet (www.padlet.com) can also be used as terms are placed on virtual sticky notes and then moved around in clusters to create categories. On the iPad, applications like Explain Everything or Skitch can serve as a whiteboard for recording student lists.

Text Type
Narrative
Informational

Disciplinary Considerations
♦ Building prior knowledge
♦ Building specialized vocabulary
♦ Learning to deconstruct complex sentences
♦ Using knowledge of text structures and genres to predict main and subordinate ideas
♦ Posing discipline-relevant questions

Common Core Anchor Standards
Reading
♦ Analyze the structure of texts, including how specific sentences, paragraphs, and larger portions of the text (e.g., a section, chapter, scene, or stanza) relate to each other and the whole.
♦ Assess how point of view or purpose shapes the content and style of a text.

Strategic Behaviors
Using Prior Knowledge
Asking Questions
Inferring
Determining Importance
Synthesizing

Suggested Uses for Disciplinary Literacy
ELA: Have students generate lists of character attributes or themes from a work of literature and organize them into logical categories.

History: Have students generate lists of evidence to support a particular historical claim and organize the evidence into broader categories that reflect interpretive lenses.

Science: Have students generate lists of categories or properties and organize them into superordinate categories.

Math: Have students generate lists of algebraic or geometric properties and organize them into logical categories.

Procedure

1. Choose a major concept or topic being studied by the class. In an Earth Science class, a key topic might be minerals.

2. Ask students to brainstorm words related to the topic. For example, words related to earth's materials might include *zinc, quartz, aluminum, bauxite, cobalt, copper, lead,* and *nickel.* Try to keep the number of responses to 20–25 for ease of management.

3. When the brainstormed words have been listed, read them aloud and ask students to cluster the terms into smaller groups based on shared relationships or characteristics. This can be done in list form (see the List-Group-Label reproducible on page 57) or in graphic form (see reproducible on page 105). Students should label clusters or give them titles to indicate what the terms have in common. You may wish to have students complete this step in small cooperative groups. It is often possible for some of the brainstormed words to become category headings. Examples of the labels for clusters related to minerals might be *Oxides, Silicates, Carbonates, Sulfates,* and *Phosphates.*

4. When students have completed their classification and categorization of the words, invite students to share the labels for each of their clusters and the words they have included under each heading. You may wish to record these where they can be viewed by students.

5. It is important for students to share their *reasoning* for their cluster decisions. This sharing stimulates students to think of the words in a variety of ways, consider their meanings, connect them, and see relationships between and among the words. A List-Group-Label sample is found on page 56.

6. If used as an activity to activate prior knowledge, direct students to use the text to confirm or refute their classifications. They may need to rearrange some words based on additional information in the lesson.

7. If used as a summary task after an initial reading, students should revisit the text to confirm the reasoning for, and accuracy of, their clusters. Students may also wish to use their completed lists or semantic maps as a study aid.

8. When the lists or semantic maps are complete, have students work individually or in pairs to write a summary of the information in one of the clusters or write a longer piece about the topic, using each one of the clusters of information as a paragraph in the longer piece.

Additional Considerations for Successful Implementation

♦ The strategy work can be extended over the course of several days as students acquire additional information about the topic. More words can be added to the clusters as students build their knowledge base and increase the connections they make between and among the words.

♦ If desired, colored inks or highlighters can be used for terms added from additional sources or at different times, thus graphically illustrating the expanding knowledge base for the students and the desirability of using a variety of resources in acquiring information.

References

Heimlich, J. E., & Pittelman, S. D. (1986). *Semantic mapping: Classroom applications.* Newark, DE: International Reading Association.

Johnson, D. D., & Pearson, P. D. (1984). *Teaching reading vocabulary* (2nd ed.). New York, NY: Holt, Rinehart, & Winston.

Pearson, P. D., & Johnson, D. D. (1978). *Teaching reading comprehension.* New York, NY: Holt, Rinehart, & Winston.

Taba, H. (1967). *Teacher's handbook for elementary social studies.* Reading, MA: Addison-Wesley.

_____ *Nervous System* _____
(topic)

1. Brainstorm a list of words related to the topic given to you by your teacher. Write the topic on the line above and list the words that are related to it in the space below.

brain	*brain stem*	*autonomic*
somatic	*sympathetic*	*reflexes*
cerebellum	*spinal cord*	*parasympathetic*
cerebrum	*meninges*	*nerves*

2. Now consider how some of the words listed above might be related. Think of ways they might be grouped together by their meanings. Write the title of the categories or headings on each line below. (You may have a greater or lesser number of words and groupings than the number of lines below.) Then list the words under the appropriate headings. Use the back of this paper for additional words and clusters if you need it.

Central Nervous System	*Peripheral Nervous System*
(cluster heading)	(cluster heading)
1. *brain*	1. *autonomic*
2. *spinal cord*	2. *somatic*
3. *cerebellum*	3. *sympathetic*
4. *cerebrum*	4. *parasympathetic*
5. *brain stem*	5. *reflexes*
6. *meninges*	6. *nerves*

List-Group-Label

_____
(topic)

1. Brainstorm a list of words related to the topic given to you by your teacher. Write the topic on the line above and list the words that are related to it in the space below.

2. Now consider how some of the words listed above might be related. Think of ways they might be grouped together by their meanings. Write the title of the categories or headings on each line below. (You may have a greater or lesser number of words and groupings than the number of lines below.) Then list the words under the appropriate headings. Use the back of this paper for additional words and clusters if you need it.

| _____ | _____ |
| (cluster heading) | (cluster heading) |

1. _____
2. _____
3. _____
4. _____
5. _____

1. _____
2. _____
3. _____
4. _____
5. _____

| _____ | _____ |
| (cluster heading) | (cluster heading) |

1. _____
2. _____
3. _____
4. _____
5. _____

1. _____
2. _____
3. _____
4. _____
5. _____

Multiple-Text GIST

Description

Multiple-Text GIST (Manderino, 2007) is adapted for multiple texts from the GIST strategy designed for single texts (Cunningham, 1982). Students need to work with multiple sources to develop a deeper conceptual understanding of a topic. Research (e.g., Afflerbach & VanSledright, 2001; Hynd-Shanahan, Holschuh, & Hubbard, 2004) shows that students struggle to synthesize across multiple sources without scaffolding. Multiple-Text GIST is a strategy designed to scaffold student thinking across multiple sources and source types. It is especially useful with documents that are contradictory. As students read each text, they write an integrative summary that builds as they read each text.

Bridge to the Disciplines

Multiple-Text GIST can be used to scaffold multiple text synthesis of contradictory texts. The strategy helps support disciplinary literacy by scaffolding the ways students reconcile texts that are contradictory, corroborated, or unique. Having students summarize across texts is a first step to their synthesis and argument creation across multiple texts. Deep disciplinary learning requires that students use multiple sources of information that need to be reconciled in order to generate their own knowledge.

Technology Connections

Multiple-Text GIST can easily be adapted for use in shared platforms like Google Drive or Evernote. Multiple-Text GIST is also ideal for students to use when reading multimedia sources in combination with print resources.

Text Type
Narrative
Informational

Disciplinary Considerations
- Building prior knowledge
- Comparing claims and propositions across texts
- Using norms for reasoning within the discipline (i.e., what counts as evidence) to evaluate claims

Common Core Anchor Standards
Reading
- Integrate and evaluate content presented in diverse media and formats, including visually and quantitatively, as well as in words.
- Analyze how two or more texts address similar themes or topics in order to build knowledge or to compare the approaches the authors take.

Writing
- Gather relevant information from multiple print and digital sources, assess the credibility and accuracy of each source, and integrate the information while avoiding plagiarism.

Strategic Behaviors
Monitoring Meaning
Using Prior Knowledge
Inferring
Determining Importance
Synthesizing

Suggested Uses for Disciplinary Literacy
ELA: Provide students with four or five literary non-fiction texts that offer multiple interpretations of a single work of literature.

History: Provide students with an inquiry question and competing sources that address the question.

Science: Have students summarize multiple texts that address a science topic that requires an in-depth explanation.

Math: Provide students with multiple texts that that lead to a complete conceptual understanding of a topic.

Procedure

1. Duplicate copies of the reproducible on page 61 or have students create a template in their notebook.

2. Create a text set of four to eight sources on a topic. Sources can be contradictory, unique, or corroborate information from different viewpoints.

3. Read aloud the first text and model how to write a 20-word summary of the text. It is helpful to model by thinking through the process aloud and not just sharing a prewritten summary you created.

4. Have students read the second text and write a 20-word summary of the first and second text.

5. Encourage students to share their summaries and project examples on the board. If the second text contradicts the first text, ask students how they created their summary when the two texts were opposed. This is a good time to discuss the use of words like *despite, although,* and *however* in order to reconcile opposing texts.

6. Have students read the third text and write a 25-word summary of all three texts. Encourage students to discuss their accumulating summaries in small groups.

7. Have students read the fourth text and write a 30-word summary for all four texts. The word count is increased to accommodate the amount of text that needs to be summarized.

8. The process continues until students have read all of the texts. As the number of texts increases, you can increase the maximum amount of words used in the summary.

9. At the end of the task, project samples of students' final summaries and discuss how students made sense of the overall text set.

Additional Considerations for Successful Implementation

♦ Provide a list of words (e.g., *however, despite, although*) that can help students reconcile contradictory texts.

♦ Students can work in pairs to read the texts orally to each other or to develop their written summaries.

References

Afflerbach, P., & VanSledright, B. (2001). Hath! Doth! What? Middle graders reading innovative history text. *Journal of Adolescent & Adult Literacy, 44,* 696–707.

Cunningham, J. W. (1982). Generating interactions between schemata and text. In J. Niles & L. Harris (Eds.), *New inquiries in reading research and instruction: Thirty-first yearbook of the National Reading Conference* (pp. 42–47). Washington, DC: National Reading Conference.

Cunningham, J. W. (2013). Research on text complexity: The Common Core State Standards as catalyst. In S. B. Neuman & L. B. Gambrell (Eds.), *Quality reading instruction in the age of Common Core Standards* (pp. 136–148). Newark, DE: International Reading Association.

Hynd-Shanahan, C., Holschuh, J., & Hubbard, B. (2004). Thinking like a historian: College students' reading of multiple historical documents. *Journal of Literacy Research, 36,* 141–176.

Manderino, M. (2007, November). *Integrating the visual: Strategies for student synthesis.* Paper presented at the annual meeting of the National Reading Conference, Austin, TX.

Sample Multiple-Text GIST Strategy in **History**

Based on documents from http://sheg.stanford.edu/montgomery-bus-boycott

You should summarize each document progressively as you read through them.

Text A _____Textbook (The Montgomery Bus Boycott)_____
Summarize in 20 words or less.

Rosa Parks refused to give up her seat on a public bus and was arrested. Dr. King led a city-wide
boycott.

_____

Text B _____Letter from Robinson to the Mayor_____
Summarize Doc A + B in 20 words or less.

A year before Parks and King started the bus boycott, the Montgomery Women's Council demanded
desegregated buses.

_____

Text C _____Bayard Rustin's Diary_____
Summarize A, B, + C in 25 words or less.

The bus boycott led by King, after Parks refused to move, was widely practiced for months.

_____

Text D _____Highlander School_____
Summarize A, B, C, + D in 30 words or less.

In 1954 a group of women in Montgomery demanded bus desegregation. Rosa Parks, trained for civil
rights activism, started a large bus boycott in Montgomery led by Dr. King.

_____

Text E _____MLK_____
Summarize A, B, C, D, + E in 35 words or less.

After a struggle to desegregate busses in Montgomery by the Women's Council, Rosa Parks, a trained
civil rights leader sparked a months-long boycott led by Dr. King who promised success.

_____

Multiple-Text GIST Strategy

You should summarize each document progressively as you read through them.

Text A _____
Summarize in 20 words or less.

_____

_____

_____

Text B _____
Summarize Doc A + B in 20 words or less.

_____

_____

_____

Text C _____
Summarize A, B, + C in 25 words or less.

_____

_____

_____

Text D _____
Summarize A, B, C, + D in 30 words or less.

_____

_____

_____

Text E _____
Summarize A, B, C, D, + E in 35 words or less.

_____

_____

_____

_____

Observation-Inference Chart

Description

The Observation-Inference Chart (Nokes, 2008) is an organizational scaffold for distinguishing between one's observations and the corresponding inferences one makes about a particular observation. The strategy is particularly designed for use with non-print texts (e.g., photographs, cartoons, videos, or lab demonstrations).

Bridge to the Disciplines

Non-traditional texts are an integral part of the multitude of texts that are used in the disciplines. Students' ability to analyze and construct meaning from these types of texts is critical to possessing a more complete conceptual understanding in a discipline. This scaffold is an important step for students to actively make inferences from non-traditional texts that are often vital to understanding corresponding written text as well. The Observation-Inference Chart can also be modified to fit the discipline. For example, in science, columns can be added to develop a hypothesis from the inferences that are made.

Technology Connections

Non-traditional texts that are commonly found online are ideal to analyze using an Observation-Inference Chart. Observation-Inference Charts can easily be created using Google Docs or with an online whiteboard iPad application like Explain Everything.

Text Type
Narrative
Informational (especially non-print sources)

Disciplinary Considerations
- Close reading
- Using knowledge of text structures and genres to predict main and subordinate ideas
- Using norms for reasoning within the discipline (i.e., what counts as evidence) to evaluate claims

Common Core Anchor Standards
Reading
- Read closely to determine what the text says explicitly and to make logical inferences from it; cite specific textual evidence when writing or speaking to support conclusions drawn from the text.

Strategic Behaviors
Inferring
Determining Importance

Suggested Uses for Disciplinary Literacy
ELA: Have students analyze an iconic photograph or scene from a visual adaptation like a graphic novel or video.

History: Have students analyze a map or political cartoon.

Science: Have students analyze a lab demonstration or diagram of a process.

Math: Have students analyze a geometric representation or real-world visual example of a mathematical principle.

Procedures

1. Select a non-print source for students to analyze. Examples might include a photograph, artwork, political cartoon, figure, or diagram, or dynamic text like a lab demonstration or video.

2. Duplicate the reproducible on page 64 or have students create an Observation-Inference Chart in their notebooks or electronically.

3. Model initial observations from the text. For example, using a photograph of student sit-ins in the 1960s, you could write an observation that African-American students were sitting at a lunch counter with no food in front of them. A second observation could be that only African-Americans are sitting along the entire lunch counter. Then you would model the inference that the restaurant refused service to these students. Another inference might be that the sit-ins were planned by young African-American men and women. You should also draw arrows from the observation to the inference.

© Bettmann/Corbis

4. Have students continue in small groups making additional observations and inferences and drawing connecting arrows between their observations and inferences about a particular observation. Circulate among the groups and provide assistance as necessary.

5. Students individually write an overall interpretation about the meaning or significance of the text based on their observations and inferences.

6. Come back together as a whole class and share observations and inferences about the source.

Additional Suggestions for Successful Implementation

♦ You can add a column to have students support their inference with text evidence (see reproducible on page 65).

♦ Add a column in science to include observation/inference/hypothesis (see reproducible on page 64).

Reference

Nokes, J. D. (2008). The Observation/Inference Chart: Improving students' abilities to make inferences while reading nontraditional texts. *Journal of Adolescent & Adult Literacy, 51*, 538–546.

Observation-Inference Chart

Text: _____

Observation	Inference

Summary:

Observation-Inference/Evidence Chart

Text: _____

Observation	Inference	Text Evidence

Summary:

Plot/Concept Relationships

Description

Originally called the Plot Relationships chart (Schmidt & Buckley, 1991), this strategy can be used with narrative text to teach story grammar and with informational text to teach students cause-effect relationships. When students complete the Plot/Concept Relationships chart, they are visually representing the connections between characters and stories, events in history, hierarchical concepts in science, or steps of inquiry in math and science.

Bridge to the Disciplines

Each discipline uses different text structures to organize and communicate meaning. Plot/Concept Relationships provide scaffolds for student understanding of how authors in a discipline communicate meaning.

Technology Connections

Students can construct their own Plot/Concept Relationships using online whiteboards from sites like www.bubbl.us, www.dabbleboard.com, and www.mindomo.com. On the iPad, whiteboard applications like Explain Everything or Skitch can also be used to construct Plot/Concept Relationships.

Text Type
Narrative
Informational

Disciplinary Considerations
- Building prior knowledge
- Using knowledge of text structures and genres to predict main and subordinate ideas
- Causal reasoning

Common Core Anchor Standards
Reading
- Analyze the structure of texts, including how specific sentences, paragraphs, and larger portions of the text (e.g., a section, chapter, scene, or stanza) relate to each other and the whole.

Strategic Behaviors
Using Prior Knowledge
Creating Images
Determining Importance

Suggested Uses for Disciplinary Literacy
ELA: Have students create story maps to analyze for plot structure. This analysis can lead to later discussion about how the author developed ideas across the text.

History: Have students construct cause-effect maps to identify causal vs. coincidental relationships of an event.

Science: Have students create cause-effect maps for a causal scientific phenomenon.

Math: Have students create concept maps for the steps to solving a problem.

Procedure

1. To teach Plot/Concept Relationships, choose a story that has clear elements of plot such as characters, goal, problem, and solution. To teach cause-effect relationships, choose an informational text that has clear examples of the events that lead to other events. For example, have students map the events leading to Haiti's independence from France. To teach scientific concepts or steps of inquiry, choose a science text that has clear conceptual definitions or that states procedural steps of inquiry.

2. Use an example you develop for the sample Plot/Concept Relationships chart on page 67. Model for students how to use this strategy.

3. Display and duplicate copies of the Plot/Concept Relationships reproducible on page 68 or adapt it to suit your needs or purposes.

4. To model Plot/Concept Relationships, review with students the basic elements of the story: stories usually have main characters, goals the characters wish to achieve, problems that prevent them from achieving the goal, and a solution to the problem. In the sample Plot/Concept Relationships chart below, a story from a middle school literature anthology is used.

5. Read through the four boxes in the sample with students. Ask them to generate full sentences using the information in all four boxes. For example, "Carlos wanted to buy a new camera lens, but he did not have enough money, so he had to work more hours to earn the money."

Sample Plot Relationships for **Literature**

Somebody	Wanted	But	So
Carlos	to buy a new camera lens	he didn't have enough money	he had to work more hours to earn the money

Carlos wanted to buy a new camera lens, but he didn't have enough money, so he had to work more hours to earn the money.

6. Instruct students to read the story you chose for them and to use the strategy to first complete the four boxes. Then have students write out the complete sentence containing the basic information.

7. To model Concept Relationships, review with students how to determine cause and effect, looking for key-words such as *because, when*, and *if-then*.

8. Read through the four boxes in the sample with students and ask them to generate full sentences using the information in all four boxes. For example, in a science sample, students might write: "Because humans are warm-blooded and breathe by lungs and sharks are cold-blooded and breathe by gills, humans are different from sharks."

9. Move on to the informational text you choose for the students. Instruct students to use the strategy to first complete the four boxes and then write out the complete sentence.

10. Demonstrate another type of Concept Relationships chart with headings of "problem," "hypothesis," "test-ing," and "conclusion." For example, when a question is posed in science, the second chart is more appropri-ate. When a cause-and-effect relationship is delineated, the first chart is more appropriate.

11. Encourage students to use a Plot/Concept Relationships chart whenever they need to demonstrate compre-hension of text. Reproducibles can be found on pages 68–69.

Additional Considerations for Successful Implementation

♦ Add a summary at the end of the Plot/Concept Relationships chart to help students convey their disciplinary reasoning.

Reference

Schmidt, B., & Buckley, M. (1991). Plot relationships chart. In J. M. Macon, D. Bewell, & M. Vogt (Eds.), *Responses to literature: Grades K–8* (pp. 7–8). Newark, DE: International Reading Association.

Plot/Concept Relationships

Somebody	Wanted	But	So

_____

_____

_____

_____

_____

_____

_____

_____

Concept Relationships

Problem	Hypothesis	Testing	Conclusion

_____

_____

_____

_____

_____

_____

_____

_____

Possible Sentences

Description

Possible Sentences (Moore & Moore, 1992; Readence, Bean, & Baldwin, 2011) is used to help students predict the content in a lesson and then check their predictions while reading. After reading, students use the text and other sources to judge the accuracy of their predictions or revise them so they are more reflective of the content of the lesson. This strategy helps students to set a purpose for reading as well as to develop interest in and curiosity about the text. Through its use, students formulate questions that they wish to answer, make connections to their background knowledge, and, based on the vocabulary selected, make inferences about the content of the lesson.

Bridge to the Disciplines

Language in the disciplines is used for specific purposes. Generating Possible Sentences and then checking them helps students become familiar with the writing style of the discipline as well as the use of some of the key vocabulary. Students also need to read closely to determine the accuracy of their sentences and revise, when necessary, after checking them against the text.

Technology Connections

Students can generate Possible Sentences to be shared using online sticky notes via Padlet (www.padlet.com) or using Today's Meet (www.todaysmeet.com). By sharing their generated sentences with the whole class, students gain feedback quickly and can revise if necessary.

Text Type
Narrative
Informational

Disciplinary Considerations
♦ Close reading
♦ Building prior knowledge
♦ Building specialized vocabulary
♦ Learning to deconstruct complex sentences
♦ Posing discipline-relevant questions

Common Core Anchor Standards
Reading
♦ Read closely to determine what the text says explicitly and to make logical inferences from it; cite specific textual evidence . . . drawn from the text.
♦ Read and comprehend complex literary and informational texts.

Strategic Behaviors
Using Prior Knowledge
Inferring
Synthesizing

Suggested Uses for Disciplinary Literacy

ELA: In helping students understand the dramatic structure in a short story, use these words in a Possible Sentence activity: *exposition, conflict, antagonist, resolution, protagonist, setting, obstacles, climax.*

History: Before reading several documents from a variety of sources regarding the causes of a particular war, ask students to write sentences using these words: *assaulted, uprising, dissent, resources, industrial workers, aggression, capitalists.*

Science: In an introductory lesson on the Internet, ask students to create sentences using the following words: *network, URL, graphic, AUP, modem, webpage, text, ISP, hyperlink, web browser.*

Math: As an introduction to inverse functions, have students write sentences using one or two of the following words in each sentence: *direction, algorithm, quantity, function, operation, inverse, radical, undoing, values, backward.*

Procedure

1. Display 10–15 key vocabulary words (some new, some familiar) from a text selection. Pronounce the words for students.

2. Ask students to select words from the list and use them in sentences that they believe might appear in the selection. Stress that students should use their prior knowledge about the words. Encourage students to write their sentences on their personal electronic devices or on the reproducible on page 72. Remind students and stress that their sentences should be those that they might expect to see in the text as they read.

3. Ask students to share their sentences orally. Note words from the list as they are used. Continue until all the words have been used or until the available time has elapsed.

4. Have students read the text, passage, or selection.

5. After reading, have students reread each sentence they created and determine its accuracy. Rate it T (true), F (false), or DK (don't know; not enough information given).

6. Revise or omit those sentences that are not accurate and those about which insufficient information was provided. Encourage students to cite specific text references in making their decisions about sentence accuracy.

7. After sentences are corrected and verified to be correct, students could be asked to enter them into their electronic notes or class log.

8. An example for social studies can be found below. A reproducible is on page 72.

Sample Possible Sentences for **Social Studies**

Ancient Rome
(topic)

Below are some words that you will find in your reading.

republic	aqueduct	disciple
dictator	persecute	census
veto	martyr	
forum	legion	

Possible Sentences

Directions: Write one or more sentences using at least two of the above terms in each sentence. Underline the words from the list above. After reading, rate the accuracy of each sentence by indicating True (T), False (F), or Don't Know (DK).

_F_ 1. One citizen became a <u>martyr</u> when he sacrificed his life rather than carry out the commands of the <u>dictator</u>.

_T_ 2. The members of the <u>forum</u> conducted a <u>census</u> of the population to determine the ages and locations of everyone in the <u>republic</u>.

_DK_ 3. Some of the members of the <u>legion</u> supported the building of an <u>aqueduct</u> to bring needed water to the town.

Key
T = True
F = False, needs to be rewritten
DK = Don't know, information not given in the reading

References

Moore, D. W., & Moore, S. A. (1992). Possible sentences: An update. In E. K. Dishner, T. W. Bean, J. E. Readence, & D. W. Moore (Eds.), *Reading in the content areas: Improving classroom instruction* (3rd ed., pp. 196–202). Dubuque, IA: Kendall Hunt.

Readence, J. E., Bean, T. W., & Baldwin, R. S. (2011). *Content area literacy: An integrated approach* (10th ed.). Dubuque, IA: Kendall Hunt.

Possible Sentences

_____
(topic)

Below are some words that you will find in your reading.

_____   _____   _____

_____   _____   _____

_____   _____   _____

_____   _____   _____

Possible Sentences

Directions: Write one or more sentences using at least two of the above terms in each sentence. Underline the words from the list above. After reading, rate the accuracy of each sentence by indicating True (T), False (F), or Don't Know (DK).

_____   1. _____

_____

_____   2. _____

_____

_____   3. _____

_____

_____   4. _____

_____

_____   5. _____

_____

Key

T   =   True

F   =   False, needs to be rewritten

DK =   Don't know, information not given in the reading

Question-Answer Relationships (QARs)

Description

Question-Answer Relationships (QARs) (Raphael, Highfield, & Au, 2006; Raphael & Pearson, 1982) help students to determine where and how to find answers to questions. The strategy is based on a four-part question classification system: Right There, Think and Search, Author and Me, and On My Own. These four QARs provide a helpful framework to assist students in considering the different sources they may draw on to answer questions. They also develop the ability to understand the relationship between a question and its possible answer. QARs are valuable for helping students move from using explicitly stated information to that which involves the use of implied information as well as background knowledge.

Bridge to the Disciplines

Using QARs helps students to read for information and examine and respond to texts from a variety of perspectives. In doing so, they further explore how language is structured in that specific discipline. QARs also help students learn how to study materials written in a specific discipline and how to prepare for tests in that area.

Technology Connections

Student thinking with QARs can be shared using several Web 2.0 tools such as Today's Meet (www.todaysmeet.com), Socrative (www.socrative.com), or Poll Everywhere (www.polleverywhere.com). Teachers can project the four different question types and have students respond electronically.

Text Type
Narrative
Informational

Disciplinary Considerations
♦ Building prior knowledge
♦ Learning to deconstruct complex sentences
♦ Posing discipline-relevant questions

Common Core Anchor Standards
Reading
♦ Read closely to determine what the text says explicitly and make logical inferences from it; cite specific textual evidence . . . to support conclusions drawn from the text.
♦ Read and comprehend complex literary and informational texts independently and proficiently.

Writing
♦ Use technology to produce and publish writing and to interact and collaborate with others.
♦ Draw evidence from literary or informational texts to support analysis, reflection, and research.

Strategic Behaviors
Monitoring Meaning
Using Prior Knowledge
Asking Questions
Inferring
Creating Images
Determining Importance
Synthesizing

Suggested Uses for Disciplinary Literacy
ELA: Have students develop a lesson on QARs to teach to another class or have students create questions based on a piece of literature or student-created work.

History: Have groups of students develop possible test questions based on the selection (or part of it), using all four of the question types.

Science: Have students read the questions at the end of the chapter and identify which type of question each is. Ask students to draw conclusions about which type of question is most often used by the author of their text.

Math: Have students write questions based on a current unit of study. Discuss whether all four types of questions were relevant to this information source, unit goals, and/or objectives. Which questions are more frequently used in this discipline?

Procedure

1. Ask students how they find information when they are asked to answer questions after reading. Discuss the various ways they grapple with the challenge of answering difficult questions. Are they difficult because the information is not readily available? Are they difficult because you must use your own ideas and what is already known to draw conclusions? Use this discussion to introduce QARs.

2. Provide copies of the Question-Answer Relationships (QARs) reproducible on page 75 or adapt it to suit your needs. Explain to students that as they progress through school, the types of questions they will be expected to answer become more challenging, in part because the answers come from a variety of places. You may want to display the reproducibles on pages 75 and 76 to help students understand the types of QARs.

3. Remove the answers from the copy on page 78 and distribute it or display it.

4. Read aloud the text at the top of the page and then ask the first question. Think aloud about how you will find the answer. If the answer is explicitly stated in the text, it is called a Right There question. Highlight or underline where the answer is found in the text. It is right there.

5. Read the second question aloud. Invite a student to show where the answer can be found. If the question can be answered by using information from several places in the text, it is a Think and Search question. Underline or highlight where the answer is found.

6. Invite a student to read the third question aloud. Discuss with the class the information given about cytologists and what they know about cells. (They are microscopic, so they would need a microscope to study them.) Point out that they used the information from the text (author) as well as what they know (me) about cells to answer the question, so it is an Author and Me question.

7. Invite students to read the fourth question independently and use their personal communication devices to create biological research questions. Have them share them with a partner, and finally invite whole-class sharing of some of the research questions generated. This is an example of an On My Own question.

8. After students have completed the introductory group lesson, provide students with several short reading passages accompanied by a question and an answer for each passage. Have students read each passage and identify the type of QAR represented by the answer. Invite them to justify their thinking.

9. As students become more proficient with the question types, increase the length of the practice passages.

10. Assign a reading passage and have students independently or in small groups write four questions, one for each question type, on index cards, with the correct answer on the back. Invite students or groups to exchange cards, find the answers, and see if they agree with the question types identified by the author(s).

References

Raphael, T. E., Highfield, K., & Au, K. H. (2006). *QAR now: A powerful and practical framework that develops comprehension and higher-level thinking in all students*. New York, NY: Scholastic.

Raphael, T. E., & Pearson, P. D. (1982). *The effect of metacognitive training on children's question-answering behavior*. Urbana, IL: Center for the Study of Reading.

Question-Answer Relationships (QARs)

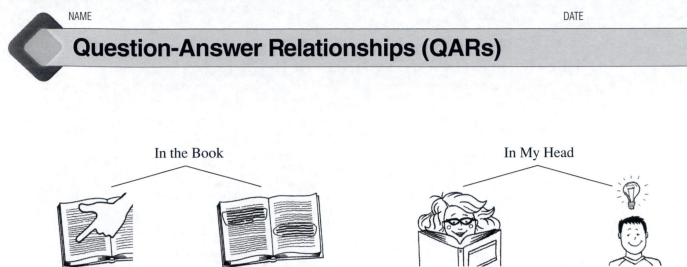

In the Book   In My Head

Right There   Think and Search   Author and Me   On My Own

In the Book Questions

Right There: The answer to the question is right in the text. You can look for key words to help you find the answer.

Think and Search: The answer is in the text, but not as easy to find. You may have to combine pieces of information from different places in the text.

In My Head Questions

Author and Me: The author may have given hints or clues that you combine with what you know to help you to figure out the answer.

On My Own: The answer is in your head. These are the questions that you really have to take time to think through. You may have to think about what you already know or about experiences you've had.

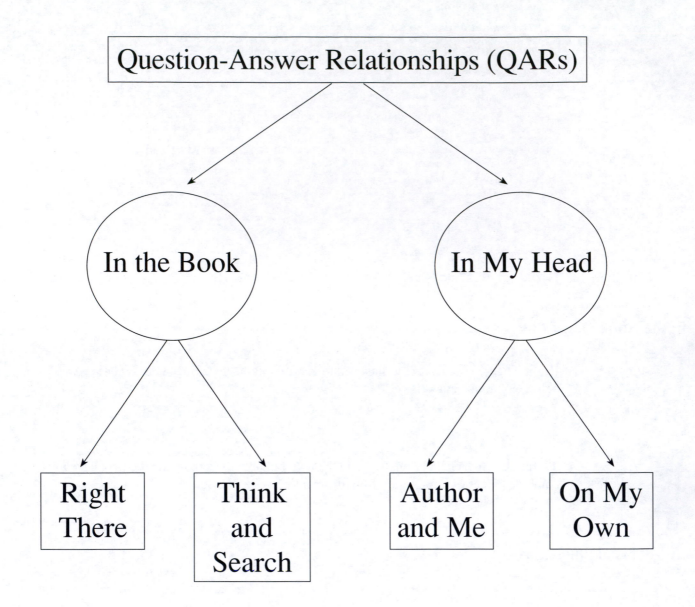

Question-Answer Relationships (QARs)

In the Book

In My Head

Right There

Think and Search

Author and Me

On My Own

Question-Answer Relationships

"Think and Search"

"Think and Search" questions usually require you to look in several parts of the text. You will need to look back at the passage, find the information that the question refers to, and then think about how the information or ideas fit together. "Think and Search" questions sometimes include the words "The main idea of the passage . . ." "What caused . . ." "Compare/contrast . . ." "How did . . ."

"On My Own"

"On My Own" questions can be answered using your background knowledge. This type of question does not usually appear on tests of reading comprehension because it does not require you to refer to the passage. "On My Own" questions sometimes include the words "In your opinion . . ." "Based on your experience . . ." "Think about someone/something you know . . ." "Would you ever . . ."

"Right There"

"Right There" questions require you to go back to the passage and find the correct information to answer the question. These are sometimes called literal questions because the correct answer can be found right there in the passage. "Right There" questions sometimes include the words "According to the passage . . ." "How many . . ." "Who is . . ." "Where is . . ." "What is . . ." "When did . . ."

"Author and Me"

"Author and Me" questions require you to use ideas and information that is not stated directly in the passage to answer the question. These questions require you to think about what you have read and what you know. Then formulate your own ideas or opinions. "Author and Me" questions sometimes include the words "The author implies . . ." "The author suggests . . ." "What did you think of . . ."

From Michael Manderino, Roberta L. Berglund, and Jerry L. Johns, *Content Area Learning: Bridges to Disciplinary Literacy* (4th ed.). Copyright © 2014 by Kendall Hunt Publishing Company (1-800-247-3458, ext. 6). May be reproduced for noncommercial educational purposes. Website: www.kendallhunt.com

The Life Sciences

Careers in life sciences can be divided into two major groups: the biology professions and the health professions. The professions in biology include many kinds of specialists who are involved in research and teaching. In general, entrance into these careers requires many years of college training plus original research.

Most biologists who study animals specialize in one group. For example, scientists called ichthyologists study fish, entomologists study insects, and herpetologists study reptiles and amphibians. Anatomists and physiologists study the structure of living organisms and the functioning of their bodies. Cytologists are biologists who study cells.

1. What are the two major groups of careers in life sciences? (Answer: RT)

 Right There   **Think and Search**   **Author and Me**   **On My Own**

2. What are three areas a biologist might choose to specialize in? (Answer: TAS)

 Right There   **Think and Search**    **Author and Me**   **On My Own**

3. What piece of equipment would be essential to a cytologist? (Answer: AAM)

 Right There    **Think and Search**    **Author and Me**   **On My Own**

4. What is one question a biologist might research? (Answer: OMO)

 Right There    **Think and Search**   **Author and Me**    **On My Own**

Role, Audience, Format, Topic (RAFT)

Description

RAFT (Role, Audience, Format, Topic) (Santa, Havens, Franciosi, & Valdes, 2014) integrates reading and writing while encouraging students to develop a deeper understanding of text. RAFT requires students to write from a perspective or viewpoint other than their own using a form that may be more unusual than common. Its purpose is to provide opportunities for students to demonstrate and communicate their understanding of a topic or subject in a creative, sometimes entertaining, way. The RAFT strategy encourages students to process information, rather than merely answer questions, and engages the audience in considering some of the key ideas and perspectives of the discipline.

Bridge to the Disciplines

Writing in the disciplines is an important step to building metacognition about the topic and how one makes sense of a topic. RAFT can be a scaffold for taking multiple perspectives in English language arts and history or providing multiple explanations of a process or topic in math and science. One goal is to use RAFT as a scaffold for students' initial writing about the content being studied.

Technology Connections

Students can write their RAFT products to be shared using Google Docs. If students are creating alternative products like a poster, they can use Glogster (www.glogster.com).

Text Type
Narrative
Informational

Disciplinary Considerations
- Building specialized vocabulary
- Learning to deconstruct complex sentences
- Using norms for reasoning within the discipline (i.e., what counts as evidence) to evaluate claims

Common Core Anchor Standards
Reading
- Read closely to determine what the text says explicitly and make logical inferences from it; cite specific textual evidence . . . to support conclusions drawn from the text.
- Determine central ideas or themes . . . summarize key supporting details and ideas.
- Read and comprehend complex literary and informational texts independently and proficiently.

Writing
- Write . . . for a range of tasks, purposes, and audiences.

Strategic Behaviors
Inferring
Determining Importance
Synthesizing

Suggested Uses for Disciplinary Literacy
ELA: Write a diary or journal from the perspective of the major protagonist sharing your thinking, feelings, and responses to events in the novel. Be sure to include text references and quotations supporting your position.

History: Assume the role of a lawyer presenting an appeal to the U.S. Supreme Court regarding a landmark court decision using text evidence.

Science: Assume the role of a major part of the circulatory system, and construct an explanatory model of your major functions.

Math: As a prime number, write instructions to the rational numbers about the rules for divisibility.

Procedure

1. Consider the major concepts or processes that you want students to learn and use in a given unit of study.

2. Consider possible roles that students might assume. See page 81 for suggested ideas.

3. Decide on possible audiences, formats, and topics that might help students extend their understanding of the key concepts, processes, and/or ideas.

4. Explain to students how all writers have to consider various aspects of writing including the role (who they are), the audience (who the reader is), the format (the writing form), and the topic (the subject or point of the piece).

5. Display a completed RAFT example using a document camera or LCD projector, if available, or read aloud some examples. Discuss the key RAFT elements with the class. Some students may appreciate clear examples of the various writing formats (e.g., travel brochures, obituaries, letters to the editor) that can be used in RAFT assignments.

6. Demonstrate, model, and think aloud another sample RAFT with the class. Brainstorm additional topics, roles, formats, and audiences that might be associated with the subject.

7. Put students into small groups. Ask them to select one role and brainstorm possible information and emotions that might be shared through the role of the writer.

8. Next, have students select their audience, format, and topic and create a group RAFT.

9. Have students share their completed RAFTs, encouraging the audience to check for accuracy of information as well as effectiveness of presentation.

10. As students gain greater competence with RAFT, they can independently write a RAFT from a chart of suggested ideas (see page 81) or create their own.

11. Because RAFT assignments vary a great deal, it is helpful to share a rubric for grading the work at the outset so that students understand the criteria on which they will be judged. Areas of the rubric might include the following: writing was appropriate for intended audience, writing followed chosen format, information presented was accurate, grammar and mechanics were acceptable. Selected areas can be weighted for greater emphasis. Be sure to star (*) these areas on the reproducible before copying and distributing it.

12. As students gain greater competence with RAFT, they can help determine what to use for the four RAFT elements (Role, Audience, Format, Topic).

Reference

Santa, C., Havens, L., Franciosi, D., & Valdes, B. (2014). *Project CRISS: Helping teachers teach and students learn* (4th ed.). Kalispell, MT: Lifelong Learning.

Sample RAFT Assignments

Role	Audience	Format	Topic
Sue, the T-Rex Dinosaur	Paleontologist	Memoir	Life in the Time of Dinosaurs
Newspaper Columnist	Jury	Testimonial	Freedom of Speech
Flight Attendant	Pilots	Proposal	Equal Pay
Chef	Cooking Class	Instructions	How to Create the Perfect Meal
Semicolon	High School Students	Complaint Letter	How It Is Misused
Meteorologist	Hurricanes	Statistics	How They Compare
Student Body President	Principal	Proposal	Reasons Why Longer Lunch Hour Needed
Naturalist John Muir	Lumber Industry	Commercial	Conservation of Natural Resources
Michelangelo	Pope	Bill	Services Provided during Painting of Sistine Chapel
Salmon	Grand Coulee Dam	Flyer	Difficulties Caused by Dam
Fraction	Whole Number	Letter	How They Are Different How They Should Work Together
Soil	Earthworm	Menu	Soil Varieties
Blood	Doctor	Travelogue	Movement through Body
Triangle	Mathematician	Appeal	Why It Is Needed
Muscles	Treadmill	Love Letter	Benefits of Exercise
Plant	Water	Thank You Note	Benefits of Water
Harry Potter	Children	Poem	The Wonders of Wizardry
Basketball	New Player	Advice Column	Tips for Success
Main Character	Students	Advice Column	Ask for help solving the conflict in the story
Cell Organelle	Boss/Employee	Resume	What I can do for the cell
MRNA	Parents/Friends	Letter from Camp	Describe protein synthesis
Sec/csc/cot	Calculator Company	Letter	Reasons to get own button on calculator
Teacher	Little Brother, Sister, or Parent	Lesson (conversation and dialogues)	Teach the concept of inertia

Sample RAFT Assignment for Students Studying the **Revolutionary War**

Directions: Consider the RAFT possibilities listed below. Choose your role and circle it. Now discuss that role with others who have selected the same one. Consider the following in your discussion.

1. Describe me.
2. What feelings do I have?
3. What information do I need to convey through my writing?
4. What words or ideas might I include to get my point across?
5. What do I know about my audience? What type of information or persuasion might they need?
6. What do I already know about the format? How might it look?

Role	Audience	Format	Topic
Young Colonist Boy	Sons of Liberty	Resume	Wants to Join
Paul Revere's Horse	Other War Horses	Memo	The Midnight Ride
Patriot Soldier	Your Family	Letter Home	Reality of War
Colonist	King	Speech	Stop Unfair Taxation
Tea	Colonists	Editorial	Stop Boston Tea Party
News Reporter	Future Generations	News Release	Tell Why Boston Massacre Was Significant
American Flag	British Citizens	Poem	Freedom

When you have finished your discussion, you may begin your work. Your RAFT assignment should be at least one page in length and will be judged using the following criteria. The starred (*) items are worth double points.

Completed on Time	1	2	3	4	5
Writing Appropriate for Audience*	1	2	3	4	5
Format Followed	1	2	3	4	5
Information Accurate*	1	2	3	4	5
Grammar and Mechanics	1	2	3	4	5
Neatness	1	2	3	4	5
Creativity	1	2	3	4	5

RAFT

Directions: Consider the RAFT possibilities listed below. Choose your role and circle it. Now discuss that role with others who have selected the same one. Consider the following in your discussion.

1. Describe me.
2. What feelings do I have?
3. What information do I need to convey through my writing?
4. What words or ideas might I include to get my point across?
5. What do I know about my audience? What type of information or persuasion might they need?
6. What do I already know about the format? How might it look?

Role	Audience	Format	Topic

When you have finished your discussion, you may begin your work. Your RAFT assignment should be at least one page in length and will be judged using the following criteria. The starred (*) items are worth double points.

Completed on Time	1	2	3	4	5
Writing Appropriate for Audience	1	2	3	4	5
Format Followed	1	2	3	4	5
Information Accurate	1	2	3	4	5
Grammar and Mechanics	1	2	3	4	5
Neatness	1	2	3	4	5
Creativity	1	2	3	4	5

RAFT Rubric

Role _____   **Format** _____

Audience _____   **Topic** _____

Completed on Time	1	2	3	4	5
Writing Appropriate for Audience	1	2	3	4	5
Format Followed	1	2	3	4	5
Information Accurate	1	2	3	4	5
Grammar and Mechanics	1	2	3	4	5
Neatness	1	2	3	4	5
Creativity	1	2	3	4	5
_____	1	2	3	4	5
_____	1	2	3	4	5
_____	1	2	3	4	5

Total Points _____

If items are starred (*), they are worth double points.

Save the Last Word for Me

Description

Save the Last Word for Me (Short, Harste, & Burke, 1996; Vaughan & Estes, 1986) is a useful strategy for facilitating text-based discussions in the disciplines. With this strategy, students are encouraged to take an active role in selecting and responding to sections of a text. They then have an opportunity to discuss their choices with other students. One of the advantages of Save the Last Word for Me is that everyone has an opportunity to comment before the student who shares the quote has an opportunity to comment about it. This procedure allows the student to consider additional ideas and to add to or delete ideas from his or her original response prior to sharing it with others.

Bridge to the Disciplines

Save the Last Word for Me provides students the opportunity to engage in close disciplinary reading. The strategy can be used to interrogate the author's claims and the use of evidence to support those claims, which are vital to critiquing disciplinary constructions of knowledge. Save the Last Word for Me also scaffolds students' text-based discussions by focusing them back to the text.

Technology Connections

Save the Last Word for Me can be adapted in a web environment using quizlet.com to create online notecards. Students could also use Today's Meet (www.todaysmeet.com) to facilitate the strategy online. Students could post the text quotations, the group members could respond using the Today's Meet platform, and then the initiators could provide responses integrating the ideas of the group.

Text Type
Narrative
Informational

Disciplinary Considerations
- Building prior knowledge
- Building specialized vocabulary
- Using norms for reasoning within the discipline (i.e., what counts as evidence) to evaluate claims

Common Core Anchor Standards
Reading
- Analyze the structure of texts, including how specific sentences, paragraphs, and larger portions of the text (e.g., a section, chapter, scene, or stanza) relate to each other and the whole.
- Assess how point of view or purpose shapes the content and style of a text.

Strategic Behaviors
Using Prior Knowledge
Asking Questions
Inferring
Determining Importance
Synthesizing

Suggested Uses for Disciplinary Literacy
ELA: Have students identify key passages of text where an author uses a particular literary device (e.g., symbolism, metaphor, personification).

History: Have students identify central assertions made by the author and evaluate why the claim is grounded in evidence.

Science: Have students identify key passages of text that provide evidence in support of a scientific model or hypothesis.

Math: Have students read example problems and identify the process they used to solve the problem.

Procedure

1. Distribute three 3x5-inch cards to each student, or make copies of the Save the Last Word for Me reproducible on page 88 and distribute one to each student.

2. Have each student read the selected text independently.

3. As students read, have them lightly mark with pencil sentences or small sections of the text about which they have a reaction, question, or connection. See the discipline-specific examples on the previous page.

4. After reading, have students select three of the sentences or sections of text they have marked and write each on an index card or on their copy of the Save the Last Word for Me reproducible.

5. Students then need to write their comments and thoughts about each of the text segments on the backs of the cards or on the Save the Last Word for Me reproducible. When this task is completed, place students in groups of four or five. You may want to display the Discussion Guide on page 89 and use it to highlight the procedures that follow. The Discussion Guide can be referred to as students share.

6. Choose one student in each group to begin. That student reads one of the text segments he or she has selected. Only the text segment is shared at this time.

7. Each member of the group is then invited to comment on the first student's text segment or quote.

8. When all students in the group have commented, the student who shared the quote offers his or her comments about it. The comments may or may not be the same as the original thoughts or ideas written.

9. The process continues by having another student share a quote from one of the cards or the Save the Last Word for Me reproducible.

10. At the conclusion of the lesson, ask students if selecting the sentences and discussing them helped them understand the text. Stress that making connections, asking questions, identifying confusing passages, and reacting during reading can aid students' understanding of the selection. A completed example is found on page 87.

Additional Considerations for Successful Implementation

♦ Have students use the strategy to revisit a reading completed for homework.

♦ Initially, you may want to select a particular quote or text segment for the whole class to analyze or react to.

References

Short, K. G., Harste, J. C.. & Burke, C. (1996). *Creating classrooms for authors and inquirers* (2nd ed.). Portsmouth, NH: Heinemann.
Vaughan, J. L., & Estes, T. H. (1986). *Reading and reasoning beyond the primary grades*. Boston, MA: Allyn & Bacon.

Directions: As you read, make a light mark with your pencil next to three statements in the text that *represent important steps in the process* of *Coping with Loss*. When you finish reading, write each statement in one of the boxes below. Then write your reasoning for choosing that statement. You might include questions or personal connections you have as well. When you finish, you will have the opportunity to discuss the text with a small group of your classmates.

Title: *Coping with Loss*

My first quote, page *228*

Any loss requires change and that change can be stressful.

My reasoning for selecting this quote:

An important part of the process is recognizing that change will occur. One needs to expect that loss will cause stress.

My second quote, page *229*

Hope operates through all five stages of grief.

My reasoning for selecting this quote:

There are five stages of grief. Hope is an important part of each stage.

My third quote, page *230*

What helped me most was talking to my family.

My reasoning for selecting this quote:

Talking is an important part of the process for coping with loss. Other important parts of the process include acceptance and seeking the comfort of others.

Save the Last Word for Me

Directions: As you read, make a light mark with your pencil next to three statements in the passage that you either agree with, disagree with, connect with, or wish to comment about. When you finish reading, write each statement in one of the boxes below. Then write your comments below it. You might include questions or thoughts you have about each of the quotes. When you finish, you will have the opportunity to discuss the text with a small group of your classmates.

Title: _____

My first quote, page _____

My reasoning for selecting this quote:

My second quote, page _____

My reasoning for selecting this quote:

My third quote, page _____

My reasoning for selecting this quote:

1 Choose someone to begin.

2 Have the first person read his or her first quote, but make no comment about it.

3 Moving around the circle, have each member of the group take a turn in commenting about the first person's quote.

4 When each person has had a chance to comment, the person who chose the quote may then share his or her comment about the quote. This may be a combination of what was written on the card as well as a response to what was said during the discussion.

5 Select another member of the group to read a quote.

6 Continue the reading and commenting until all quotes and comments have been made.

7 Remember that the person who shares a quote needs to be the **last** one to make comments about it. In other words, "Save the last word for me!"

Say Something

Description

Say Something (Beers, 2003; Short, Harste, & Burke, 1996) offers opportunities for students to respond to text during rather than after reading. The strategy highlights the social nature of language by offering students the opportunity to share their thinking with a partner or partners. At pre-selected stopping points in the reading, students make connections between the text and their own experiences and briefly discuss what the passage means to them. Students may also make predictions about the next text segment, pose questions, ask for clarification from their partner(s), or offer a response related to the text. When students are required to Say Something, they tend to read the text more closely. Proficient readers often carry on a running monologue in their heads while reading, chunking text, posing questions, making predictions, and responding to ideas. Through the use of Say Something, students are likely stimulated to become more engaged in the reading process and aware of effective strategies to use when reading independently.

Bridge to the Disciplines

Providing opportunities for students to become comfortable with commenting on a single text leads to richer and more in-depth analysis across several information sources. It also offers students opportunities to think about the claim the author is making and how that claim is supported.

Technology Connections

Students can audio-record their Say Something responses on an iPod or iPad for future reference. Students can share their Say Something responses collaboratively using Voicethread (www.voicethread.com).

Text Type
Narrative
Informational

Disciplinary Considerations
- Building prior knowledge
- Posing discipline-relevant questions
- Using norms for reasoning within the discipline (i.e., what counts as evidence) to evaluate claims

Common Core Anchor Standards
Reading
- Read closely to determine what the text says explicitly and to make logical inferences from it; cite specific textual evidence when writing or speaking to support conclusions drawn from the text.
- Delineate and evaluate the argument and specific claims in the text, including the validity of the reasoning as well as the relevance and sufficiency of the evidence.
- Read and comprehend complex literary and informational texts independently and proficiently.

Speaking and Listening
- Prepare for and participate effectively in a range of conversations and collaborations with diverse partners.
- Present information . . . such that listeners can follow the line of reasoning.

Strategic Behaviors
Using Prior Knowledge
Asking Questions
Inferring
Synthesizing

Suggested Uses for Disciplinary Literacy
ELA: Choose stopping points corresponding to important events in a short story or novel and have students Say Something to their shoulder partner.

History: Show a video of an historical or current event. Choose critical stopping points and ask students to write a comment or question.

Science: Ask students to work with a partner and follow the steps in an experiment. Prior to each step, ask them to write a prediction in their science journals. Following each step, have students write a comment.

Math: When learning a mathematical process, set a timer and have students stop and check in with a partner regarding their progress, questions, confusions, and understandings. Monitor the comments and use them as an informal guide to how well students are demonstrating understanding and confidence or if re-teaching is needed.

Procedure

1. Select a reading passage and logical stopping points. Paragraphs and sections of text with subheadings make good stopping points.

2. Invite students to choose a partner or designate partners.

3. Provide each partner team access to the text selection.

4. Invite each team to decide how they will read the selection—silently or aloud.

5. To introduce the strategy, demonstrate the Say Something process with another student or colleague, using the first segment or two of the selection.

6. When students appear to understand how to engage in the process, invite them to read to the next stopping point and Say Something to their partner(s) about the reading. Suggestions for beginning Say Something prompts to help students successfully participate are found on page 92.

7. Emphasize that responses and interpretations are acceptable if the student can support the position.

8. When students complete the reading of the selection, conduct a discussion of the process and the content.

9. Create a list of strategies students used while engaging in the strategy.

10. Help students understand how they can use the strategies of using prior knowledge, questioning, inferring, and synthesizing when they are reading independently.

Additional Considerations for Successful Implementation

♦ For less proficient readers, start with shorter text.

♦ For English Language Learners, provide the suggested sentence stems on page 92. Perhaps suggest that students narrow their responses to one type (prediction, question, clarification, connection, or comment) until they have learned to use all of them.

♦ Create discipline-specific prompts. An example in History might be, *This source corroborates with . . .* or an example in Science might be, *My initial hypothesis is that . . .*

♦ Writing can be substituted for oral response.

♦ Students who find they have little or nothing to say need to reread the text.

♦ Post the Rules for Say Something in the classroom.

© Rido, 2014. Under license from Shutterstock, Inc.

References

Beers, K. (2003). *When kids can't read: What teachers can do.* Portsmouth, NH: Heinemann.

Short, K. G., Harste, J. C., & Burke, C. (1996). *Creating classrooms for authors and inquirers* (2nd ed.). Portsmouth, NH: Heinemann.

Say Something

When working with your partner(s), you might select from the following ideas to form your comments.

Make a Connection

- This reminds me of . . .
- This character makes me think of . . .
- This is like something that happened to me . . .

Make a Comment

- This is confusing because . . .
- I think that . . .
- This is hard because . . .
- I like the part where . . .
- I don't like the part where . . .

Ask a Question

- Why did . . .
- I don't understand . . .
- I'm confused about . . .
- What if . . .
- Do you think that . . .
- What does this section mean?

Clarify Something You Didn't Understand

- This makes sense now . . .
- This part is really saying . . .
- At first I thought . . ., but now I think . . .
- It could mean . . .

Make a Prediction

- I think that . . .
- I predict that . . .
- Reading this part makes me think that . . . is going to happen next

Identify Arguments

- It is also important to think about . . .
- There are two sides to this argument . . .
- So, you could say . . .
- Some may think . . . others may think . . .

Select Three and Reflect (STAR)

Description

When using the Select Three and Reflect (STAR) strategy (Hoyt, 2009; Johns & Berglund, 2011), students are asked to choose three words from a recent reading selection. After choosing their words, they are asked to write an explanation for their choices. This process encourages diverse thinking, honors individual background and responses, and invites students to react to words in a way that is personal and meaningful to them.

Bridge to the Disciplines

Involving students in thinking about words in a selected text and making a connection to them helps promote understanding and engagement with the key concepts of the discipline. It also promotes careful attention to the ways that language is used to construct meaning.

Technology Connections

Students can recreate the STAR template using a whiteboard application like Explain Everything or Skitch. Students could also record their words using an online platform like Google Forms or Google Docs.

Text Type
Narrative
Informational

Disciplinary Considerations
◆ Building prior knowledge
◆ Building specialized vocabulary

Common Core Anchor Standards
Reading
◆ Read closely to determine what the text says explicitly and to make logical inferences from it; cite specific textual evidence when writing or speaking to support conclusions drawn from the text.
◆ Interpret words and phrases as they are used in a text, including technical, connotative, and figurative meanings, and analyze how specific word choices shape meaning or tone.

Speaking-Listening
◆ Prepare for and participate effectively in a range of conversations and collaborations with diverse partners.
◆ Present information . . . such that listeners can follow the line of reasoning.

Language
◆ Determine or clarify the meanings of unknown and multiple-meaning words and phrases.

Strategic Behaviors
Using Prior Knowledge
Inferring
Determining Importance

Suggested Uses for Disciplinary Literacy
ELA: Have students select a character from a novel and find quotations providing evidence for a specific character trait. Have students select words or phrases representing the author's point of view.

History: Have students select words from a primary source. Have them explain that relationship in their rationale statements in connection to the overall message of the primary source.

Science: Have students choose what they believe are the most important words in a selection and support their choices.

Math: Have students select words in a written problem that provide clues to the processes to use in solving it.

Procedure

1. Display or provide copies of the Select Three and Reflect (STAR) reproducible on page 96.

2. Ask students to review a selection or passage that has been read and then identify three interesting words found in the reading. Do not, at this time, suggest any particular criteria for selecting the words.

3. After students have had an opportunity to select their words, ask for volunteers to share the words they selected. As words are shared, write them where all students can see them.

4. Invite students to explain the reasons for their word selections. Guide students to understand that some words were chosen because they were important words in the selection, while other words may have been chosen because they connected to something in the student's life. You may also suggest that sometimes words are chosen just because they were interesting in sound or possessed some other quality. An example is given on page 95.

5. Distribute copies of the STAR reproducible or display it and have students recreate it on their personal technology devices.

6. Assign the selection to be reviewed and have students record their words and reasons for selecting them.

7. When most students have finished, have them form groups of three and share their words and their reasoning.

8. When most small groups have finished sharing, encourage volunteers to share with the whole group. Expect and reinforce both the variety of words chosen and the students' reasons for choosing them.

9. As students become familiar with the process, you may suggest criteria for selecting words that relate specifically to the content and goals of the lesson.

Additional Considerations for Successful Implementation

- Model the process from time to time by completing a STAR while students are completing theirs. Share your words and reasons for choosing them.

- Use index cards instead of the reproducible. Distribute three index cards to each student. Have them write each word on one side of a card and their reasons for selecting it on the other side.

- When sharing in small groups, be sure that each student has an opportunity to share at least one of the chosen words and rationale for selecting it.

- It often enhances interest and engagement when students find they have selected a word chosen by another student as well.

- Move from having students select words to selecting phrases from a text.

References

Hoyt, L. (2009). *Revisit, reflect, retell: Time-tested strategies for teaching reading comprehension* (updated ed.). Portsmouth, NH: Heinemann.

Johns, J. L., & Berglund, R. L. (2011). *Strategies for content area learning* (3rd ed.). Dubuque, IA: Kendall Hunt.

Sample Select Three and Reflect (STAR) for **Literature**

Directions: Choose three words from the selection and explain why you chose them. You can also explain how they relate to your reading or your life.

Title: _"Cheating Mr. Diskin"_

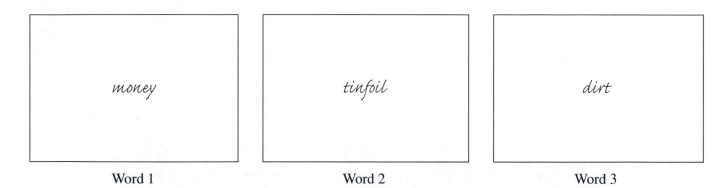

money	*tinfoil*	*dirt*
Word 1	Word 2	Word 3

Why Words Were Chosen

I chose money because the boys needed it to go to the show. They got the money by placing a stone in the tinfoil to cheat Mr. Diskin. When they went to the show, they felt like dirt. Dirt is really low.

Select Three and Reflect (STAR)

Directions: Choose three words from the selection and explain why you chose them. You can also explain how they relate to your reading or your life.

Title: _____

Word 1   Word 2   Word 3

Why Words Were Chosen

_____

_____

_____

_____

_____

_____

_____

_____

Semantic Feature Analysis (SFA)

Description

Semantic Feature Analysis (Berglund, 2002; Johnson & Pearson, 1984) is an instructional strategy that helps students identify and discriminate among the unique features of concepts or vocabulary. A classification system, in the form of a grid, helps students determine semantic similarities and differences among closely related concepts.

Bridge to the Disciplines

Disciplines have specific ways of organizing information and vocabulary. The task of completing a Semantic Feature Analysis grid helps students develop a deeper understanding of discipline-specific vocabulary and concepts and how they are organized.

Technology Connections

Semantic Feature Analysis can be used with online whiteboard applications or with a SMART Board. More contextualized examples can also be embedded by students adding links to pictures or videos showing the meaning of the words.

Text Type
Narrative
Informational

Disciplinary Considerations
- Building prior knowledge
- Building specialized vocabulary
- Posing discipline-relevant questions

Common Core Anchor Standards
Reading
- Interpret words and phrases as they are used in a text, including determining technical, commutative, and figurative meanings, and analyze how specific word choices shape meaning or tone.

Language
- Demonstrate understanding of figurative language, word relationships, and nuances in word meanings.

Strategic Behaviors
Asking Questions
Inferring
Synthesizing

Suggested Uses for Disciplinary Literacy

ELA: Students can list the major characters in a literary selection and rate them against specific traits as evidenced in the reading. This may involve making inferences about characters' motivation and reasons for their actions.

History: Listing battles and determining their influence in the outcome of a war can encourage students to ask questions, explore inferences, and synthesize information across a variety of sources.

Science: Each area of science involves many similar terms (e.g., types of gasses, states of matter) that differ in one or two critical features. Completing an SFA helps student ask questions regarding their understanding and make inferences based on the information they have explored in the text or in online resources.

Math: Students can be asked to explore the features of various quadrilaterals, for example. This encourages them to question their understanding of these terms and deepen their concept of quadrilaterals.

Procedure

1. Introduce the strategy by selecting a topic and displaying the reproducible on page 100. If students are unfamiliar with the strategy, use a topic that is familiar to many of them, for example, *Personal Technology*.

2. List words in the category down the left side of the grid. For the *Personal Technology* example, you might list *MP3 Player, Basic Phone, Smartphone, Tablet, Computer,* and *Video Game System*. Invite students to suggest additions.

3. Across the top of the chart, list features shared by some of the words in the category. The features for *Personal Technology* might be *Phone Calls, Internet, Apps, Programs, Handheld, Games,* and *Portable.*

4. Consider each word in the category relative to the features listed across the top of the grid. A plus/minus (+/−) system or a numeric system (1 = never, 2 = some, 3 = always) can be used to indicate feature possession. If the presence of the feature may be situational or dichotomous, the numerical rating system might be more useful. A question mark (?) can signal the need for more information. A plus/minus (+/−) rating indicates that the feature may be present in differing degrees or at various times. In the *Personal Technology* example, *Smartphone* would most likely receive pluses (+) for *Phone Calls, Internet, Apps, Handheld, Games,* and *Portable,* but would receive a minus (−) for *Programs*. Students should be encouraged to discuss and provide support for their ratings.

5. Complete the grid for each word in the category. You may need to add more features to the matrix in order to fully discriminate the differences among some of the words in the category.

6. When the grid is complete, ask students to examine the similarities and differences among the words in the category selected. Discuss some of their conclusions. Using the pattern of pluses and minuses, encourage students to create a summary statement regarding some of the words in the grid. For example, the summary of knowledge about personal technology might go something like this: "Personal technology devices have many similarities, including games; however, two critical differences among the devices are whether they can make and receive phone calls and whether they have the ability to access the Internet."

Additional Considerations for Successful Implementation

♦   For students who are new to this procedure, select categories that are concrete and familiar.

♦   Students may also be asked to complete the grid before and after the lesson (see page 101 for the reproducible).

♦   Students can complete the grid independently, with a learning partner, or in a small group.

♦   Discussion is critical for deeper understanding of the terms and concepts.

References

Berglund, R. L. (2002). Semantic feature analysis. In B. J. Guzzetti (Ed.), *Literacy in America: An encyclopedia of history, theory, and practice* (pp. 566–572). Santa Barbara, CA: ABC-CLIO.

Johnson, D. D., & Pearson, P. D. (1984). *Teaching reading vocabulary* (2nd ed.). New York, NY: Holt, Rinehart, & Winston.

Sample Semantic Feature Analysis (SFA) for Earth Science

Rivers and River Characteristics
(topic)

Words	Features	Caused by Erosion	Caused by Deposition	Old	Mature	Young							
Waterfalls	+	−	−	−	+								
Rapids	+	−	−	−	+								
Wide Flood Plain	+	+	+	+/−	−								
U-Shape Valley	+	−	−	−	+								
Meander	+	+	+	+	−								
Oxbow	+	−	+	−	−								
Yazoo Stream	−	+	+	−	−								
No Flood Plain	−	−	−	−	+								
Back Swamp	−	+	+	−	−								
Sand Bar	−	+	+	+	−								

Summary: *Waterfalls, rapids, wide flood plains, u-shaped valleys, meanders, and oxbows are all caused by erosion, while yazoo streams, back swamps, and sand bars are caused by deposition.*

Semantic Feature Analysis (SFA)

_____
(topic)

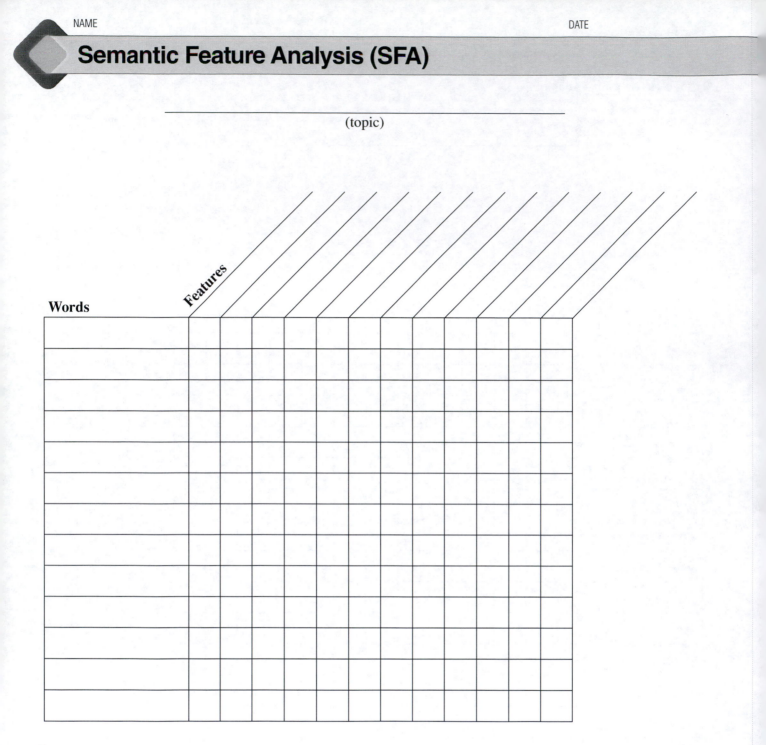

Words

Features

Summary:

Semantic Feature Analysis (SFA) Before/After

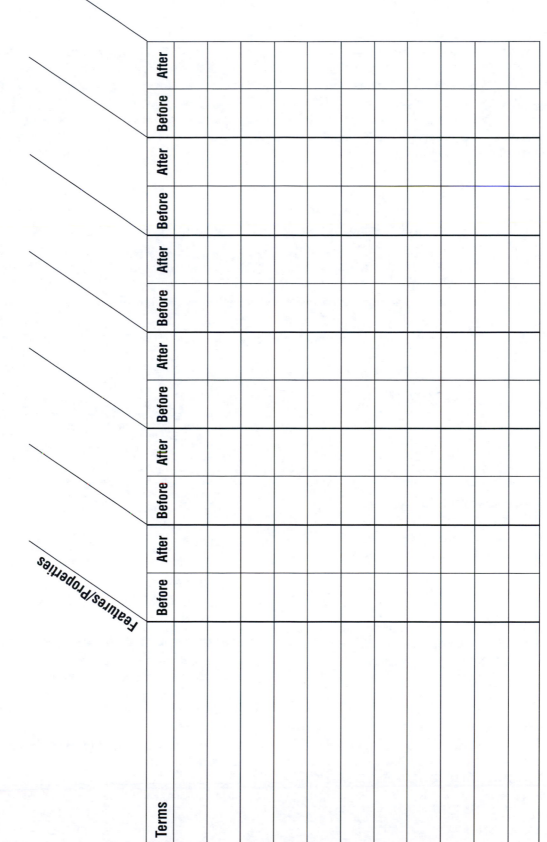

Terms	Features/Properties															
	Before	After	Before	After	Before	After	Before	After	Before	After	Before	After	Before	After

Semantic Mapping

Description

Semantic Mapping involves diagrams that show links between words and related concepts. The process helps students organize information in categorical form (Heimlich & Pittelman, 1986; Johnson & Pearson, 1984; Pearson & Johnson, 1978; Taba, 1967). By classifying and categorizing information, students become active readers and, in the process, remember new vocabulary and information. When used as a pre-reading activity, developing a Semantic Map can help activate prior knowledge and introduce key vocabulary. More information can be added during and after reading, using different colored pens, markers, or fonts to aid in identifying prior knowledge and new information.

Bridge to the Disciplines

Classifying and determining super-ordinate and subordinate ideas is an important key to conceptual understanding in most disciplines. Semantic Mapping encourages students to read and reread the text in order to add to, support, and revise their classifications.

Technology Connections

Students can use their personal communication devices with concept mapping software, available free at locations on the web: XMind (www.xmind.net) or Freemind (http://freemind.sourceforge.net/wiki/index.php/Main_Page). Web 2.0 applications include www.bubbl.us and Mindomo (www.mindomo.com).

Text Type
Narrative
Informational

Disciplinary Considerations
- Building prior knowledge
- Building specialized vocabulary
- Learning to deconstruct complex sentences
- Using knowledge of text structures and genres to predict main and subordinate ideas
- Posing discipline-relevant questions

Common Core Anchor Standards

Reading
- Read closely to determine what the text says explicitly and to make logical inferences from it; cite specific textual evidence to support conclusions drawn from the text.
- Read and comprehend complex literary and informational texts.

Writing
- Write informative/explanatory texts to examine and convey complex ideas and information clearly and accurately.
- Use technology, including the Internet, to produce and publish writing and to interact and collaborate with others.

Speaking and Listening
- Prepare for and participate effectively in a range of conversations and collaborations with diverse partners.

- Make strategic use of digital media and visual displays of data to express information and enhance understanding of presentations.

Language
- Apply knowledge of language to understand how language functions.
- Determine or clarify the meaning of unknown and multiple-meaning words.
- Acquire and use accurately a range of general academic and domain-specific words and phrases.

Strategic Behaviors
Determining Importance
Synthesizing

Suggested Uses for Disciplinary Literacy

ELA: Students can select major characters in a literary selection and identify traits related to each of them.

History: Students studying government can develop maps related to different forms of government and their characteristics.

Science: In studying geological systems in the United States, have students classify landforms.

Math: Based on a unit, for example, Measurement, have students classify terms under given headings.

Procedure

1. Choose a major concept or topic being studied by the class. In health, for example, the nervous system might be selected.

2. Put an initial list of words related to the topic on the class website or project them using the document camera, if available. Ask students to add to the list, based on their knowledge.

3. Select 20 or 25 of the words and ask students to cluster the words into smaller groups, based on shared relationships. This could be an independent assignment or done in small groups.

4. When students have completed their classification and categorization of the words, invite students to share the labels for each of their clusters and the words they have included under each heading. Suggested headings might be *Central Nervous System*, *Brain*, *Spinal Cord*, *Peripheral Nervous System*, *Autonomic*, *Somatic*. Students who have used web-based software might project their maps for the class.

5. Encourage students to share reasons for their clustering decisions. This sharing stimulates students to think of the words in a variety of ways, consider the meanings, connect them, and see relationships between and among the words.

6. If used as a pre-reading activity, ask students to access information about the nervous system and evaluate their classifications as they acquire new information. They may need to rearrange some words and add new ones, based on additional information in the lesson.

7. If used as a post-reading activity, students may want to return to the text and confirm the accuracy of their clusters. Students may also be encouraged to use their completed maps as a study aid.

8. This strategy can be used over the course of several days as students acquire additional information about the topic. It is helpful to use different colors for words added from additional sources during and after reading. This graphically illustrates the expanding knowledge base for the students and the desirability of using a variety of resources for acquiring information.

9. When the maps are complete, have students write a summary of the information in one of the clusters. Students could also write a longer piece about the topic, using each one of the clusters of information as a paragraph or section in the longer piece.

Additional Considerations for Successful Implementation

♦ Use different colors of pens or markers to identify information charted before, during, and after reading.
♦ Use different colors to identify information sources.

References

Heimlich, J. E., & Pittelman, S. D. (1986). *Semantic mapping: Classroom applications*. Newark, DE: International Reading Association.
Johnson, D. D., & Pearson, P. D. (1984). *Teaching reading vocabulary* (2nd ed.). New York, NY: Holt, Rinehart, & Winston.
Pearson, P. D., & Johnson, D. D. (1978). *Teaching reading comprehension*. New York, NY: Holt, Rinehart, & Winston.
Taba, H. (1967). *Teacher's handbook for elementary social studies*. Reading, MA: Addison-Wesley.

Sample Semantic Map Developed from a Science Lesson on the **Nervous System**

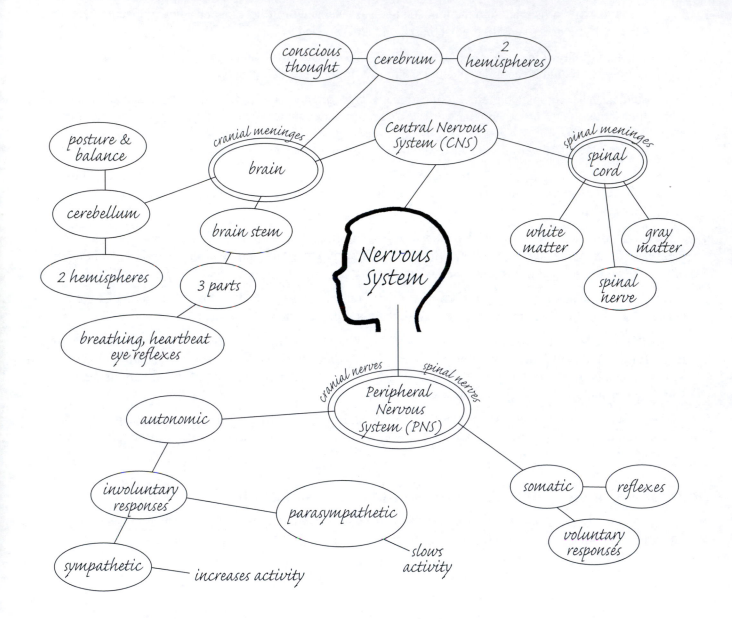

Summary: *The brain is one part of the central nervous system. Surrounded by cranial meninges, the brain has three parts: the cerebellum, the cerebrum, and the brain stem. The cerebellum has two hemispheres and controls posture and balance. The cerebrum has two hemispheres and controls conscious thought. The brain stem has three parts and controls breathing, heartbeat, and eye reflexes.*

Semantic Map

_____

(topic)

Directions: Think of ways the ideas from your lesson might be clustered together. Below is one way you might begin to cluster them into categories. You may add to the map below or create a map of your own on the back of this page.

Summary:

Synthesis Journal

Description

Students need to work with multiple sources to develop a deeper conceptual understanding of a topic. Research shows that students struggle to synthesize across multiple sources without scaffolding (e.g., Hynd-Shanahan, Holschuh, & Hubbard, 2004). The Synthesis Journal is a strategy designed to scaffold student thinking across multiple sources including their own thinking. The Journal is divided into separate sections for student notes from each source. The format validates the importance of the student's own experience and that of his or her classmates as well as that of "authority," i.e., the teacher and the author (Burrell & McAlexander, 1998).

Bridge to the Disciplines

Synthesis Journals can be used to scaffold multiple-text synthesis and comparative analysis of texts. They bridge the disciplines by scaffolding the inquiry process and providing a framework to organize information gathered from multiple sources. Deep disciplinary learning requires that students use multiple sources of information to generate their own knowledge. Synthesis Journals can be used to record assertions, main ideas and details, or relevant evidence identified in each source. They support student reading of texts that may be contradictory, complementary, or unique in order to address an inquiry question.

Technology Connections

Synthesis Journals can easily be adapted for use in shared platforms like Google Drive. Students can then collaborate or color-code claims and evidence. Other iPad apps like Scratchwork or Side-by-Side can be used. The Synthesis Journal is also ideal for students to use when reading multiple texts embedded within a single web page.

Text Type
Informational

Disciplinary Considerations
- Posing discipline-relevant questions
- Comparing claims and propositions across texts
- Using norms for reasoning within the discipline (i.e., what counts as evidence) to evaluate claims

Common Core Anchor Standards
Reading
- Integrate and evaluate content presented in diverse media and formats, including visual and quantitative, as well as in words.
- Analyze how two or more texts address similar themes or topics in order to build knowledge or to compare the approaches the authors take.

Writing
- Gather relevant information from multiple print and digital sources, assess the credibility and accuracy of each source, and integrate the information while avoiding plagiarism.

Strategic Behaviors
Monitoring Meaning
Using Prior Knowledge
Inferring
Determining Importance
Synthesizing

Suggested Uses for Disciplinary Literacy
ELA: Provide students with two or three literary non-fiction texts and have students place comparative treatments of a theme on the Synthesis Journal.

History: Provide students with competing sources on the same topic and have students record claims and evidence put forth by each source.

Science: Have students use the Synthesis Journal to record multiple data points to attempt to generate a hypothesis.

Math: Have students analyze multiple representations of data and identify variations among those representations when deciding the most appropriate way to solve a problem.

Procedures

1. Choose two or more texts that you want to use to facilitate student learning. You should consider texts that present different perspectives or different emphases of information.

2. Copy and distribute the reproducible on page 109 to each student or have them recreate the reproducible template in their notebooks.

3. Place the topic or inquiry question at the top. There are four areas for students to record information about each text. The center box is where students will place their synthesis about the inquiry question or topic (see reproducible on page 109).

4. Provide direct instruction on the topic. Have students summarize or record key ideas or claims and assertions from your instruction in the corresponding area marked "teacher says" area or box.

5. Introduce the first text. Have students summarize or record key ideas, assertions, or claims and evidence for that text in the corresponding area. You might begin by modeling your own thinking with a portion of the text. Point out the key claims or assertions made by the author.

6. Introduce the second text. Have students summarize or record key ideas, assertions, or claims and evidence for that text in the corresponding area.

7. Have students summarize their position or understanding on the topic in the remaining area.

8. Have students synthesize their response to the inquiry question for all four areas in the middle box. A completed sample for Science is on page 108.

Additional Considerations for Successful Implementation

- You can vary the order in which students give their points of view.
- You can vary when you provide direct instruction.
- You can add additional boxes if you have more sources.
- You can have students rank the sources in order of importance or relevance.
- If you want to have students synthesizing the texts in a more linear fashion, see the reproducible on page 110.

© Goodluz, 2014. Under licenses from Shutterstock, Inc.

References

Burrell, K. I., & McAlexander, P. J. (1998). Ideas in practice: The Synthesis Journal. *Journal of Developmental Education, 22,* 20–30.

Hynd-Shanahan, C., Holschuh, J. P., & Hubbard, B. P. (2004). Thinking like a historian: College students' reading of multiple historical documents. *Journal of Literacy Research, 36,* 141–176.

Sample Synthesis Journal for Science

Inquiry Question: _What causes erosion?_

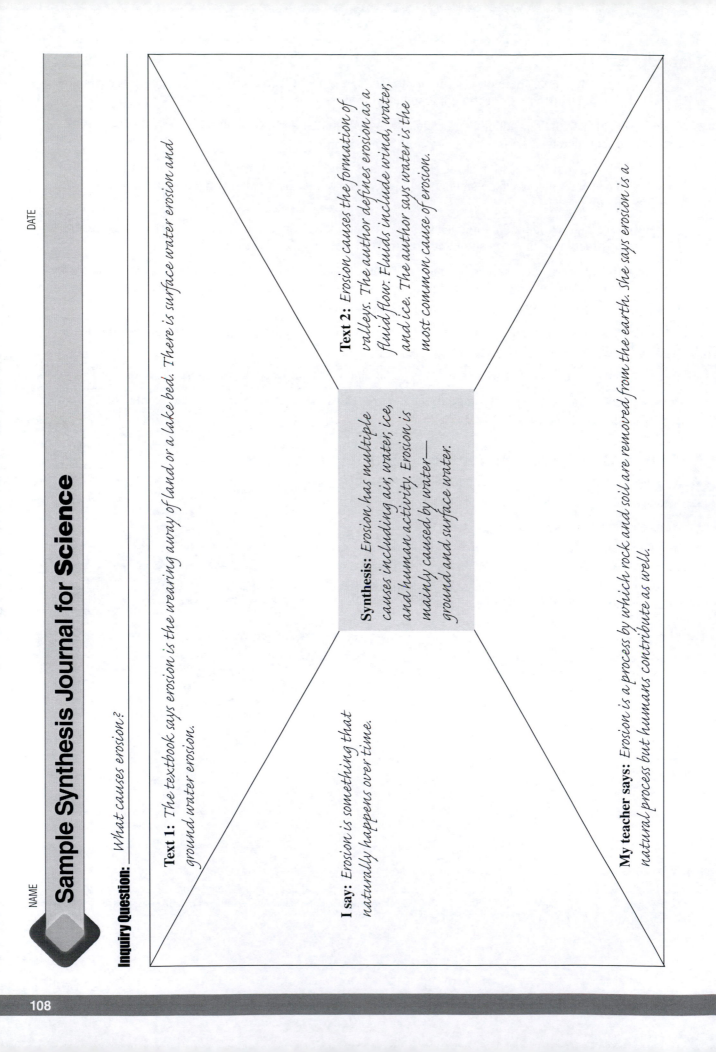

Text 1: The textbook says erosion is the wearing away of land or a lake bed. There is surface water erosion and ground water erosion.

Text 2: Erosion causes the formation of valleys. The author defines erosion as a fluid flow. Fluids include wind, water, and ice. The author says water is the most common cause of erosion.

I say: Erosion is something that naturally happens over time.

Synthesis: Erosion has multiple causes including air, water, ice, and human activity. Erosion is mainly caused by water— ground and surface water.

My teacher says: Erosion is a process by which rock and soil are removed from the earth. She says erosion is a natural process but humans contribute as well.

Synthesis Journal

Inquiry Question:

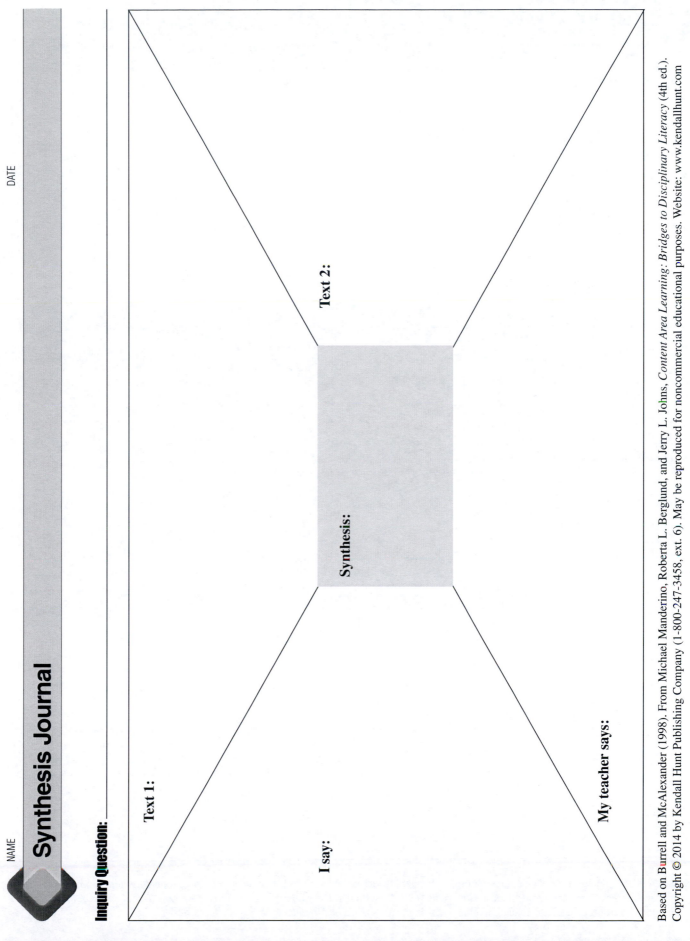

Text 1:

Text 2:

Synthesis:

I say:

My teacher says:

Based on Burrell and McAlexander (1998). From Michael Manderino, Roberta L. Berglund, and Jerry L. Johns, *Content Area Learning: Bridges to Disciplinary Literacy* (4th ed.). Copyright © 2014 by Kendall Hunt Publishing Company (1-800-247-3458, ext. 6). May be reproduced for noncommercial educational purposes. Website: www.kendallhunt.com

Synthesis Journal

My Teacher Says	Synthesis
Text 1	
Text 2	
My Partner Says	

Vocabulary Self-Collection Strategy (VSS)

Description

The Vocabulary Self-Collection Strategy (VSS) (Haggard, 1986; Ruddell & Shearer, 2002) is a simple, powerful technique to help students acquire vocabulary that is applicable to all disciplines. Central to the strategy is the practice of empowering students to determine which words the entire class will learn. Small groups of students identify vocabulary words from an assigned text and then present their "candidates" to the entire class to vote on. The strategy generates interest in words and encourages vocabulary acquisition. This strategy is especially effective for English Language Learners. Teacher modeling is critical to success.

Bridge to the Disciplines

The Vocabulary Self-Collection Strategy engages students in selecting, proposing, and arguing for studying words in any discipline. The process of developing a rationale and persuasive argument for their selection deepens students' understanding of, commitment to, and connection with the words, which often link to key concepts in the discipline. VSS helps students to understand what information is valued in that discipline.

Technology Connections

VSS templates can be created and managed in Google Forms or using Evernote; iPad apps like Skitch can be used to import a template and annotate it digitally.

Text Type
Narrative
Informational

Disciplinary Considerations
♦ Building specialized vocabulary
♦ Using norms for reasoning within the discipline (i.e., what counts as evidence) to evaluate claims

Common Core Anchor Standards
Reading
♦ Read closely to determine what the text says explicitly and make logical inferences from it; cite specific textual evidence . . . to support conclusions drawn from the text.

Speaking and Listening
♦ Prepare for and participate effectively in a range of conversations and collaborations with diverse partners, building on others' ideas and expressing their own ideas clearly and persuasively.
♦ Evaluate a speaker's point of view, reasoning, and use of evidence and rhetoric.

Language
♦ Determine or clarify the meaning of unknown words and multiple-meaning words and phrases by using context clues, analyzing meaningful word parts, and consulting general and specialized reference materials, as appropriate.

Strategic Behaviors
Inferring
Determining Importance

Suggested Uses for Disciplinary Literacy
ELA: Use VSS in playing a game called "Word Oscars." Students are asked to nominate words that fit a variety of categories, conducted in a similar format to the Academy Awards.

History: Using VSS, have students select the "Most Important Word" to learn in a particular unit of study.

Science: Using the strategy, invite students to choose words representing the essential elements of the process being studied.

Math: Use the strategy to have students select the words they believe should be on a vocabulary test related to their most recent unit of study.

Procedure

1. Display the Vocabulary Self-Collection Strategy (VSS) reproducible on page 115 to help to introduce the strategy to students. You may also want to duplicate copies for each student.

2. Model the strategy by saying, "I have reviewed the material you are about to read, and I would like to nominate one word that I think we should all learn." Write the word in the appropriate place on the reproducible.

3. Then say, "I found the word on page . . ." Write the page number in the appropriate place on the reproducible. Continue by saying, "It appeared in the following sentence." Write the sentence in which the word appears in the appropriate place on the reproducible.

4. Continue by saying, "I also used these resources to determine what the word means and found that it means . . ." Write the meaning in the appropriate place on the reproducible.

5. Then present a persuasive argument as to why this word should be learned by the entire class. Use your best sales techniques and dramatize your presentation.

6. Following the modeling, explain to the class that they will now have the opportunity to nominate words to be included on the unit vocabulary list for the entire class to study.

7. Assign the reading selection and tell students that they are each to choose one or two words from the reading that they believe should be included on the class vocabulary list. Encourage them to use a copy of the reproducible on page 114 to guide their work.

8. In a subsequent class period or when most students have finished the reading, divide the class into nominating teams of two to five students. Have them choose one person as the scribe who will complete the information on the group reproducible on page 115.

9. As students work, circulate among the groups to offer encouragement and assistance as needed. From the words offered by group members, each group should decide on one word to present to the rest of the class. They should note the page on which it is found, the sentence in which it appears, its meaning, and reasons why the entire class should learn the word.

10. When groups appear to have finished, call the class together and invite each group to present their nominated word. Usually one person does this, but sometimes each person in the group takes a different role in the presentation.

11. As each group shares a word, facilitate the discussion and write the nominated word on the board or on a chart with consensus meanings. Encourage additional clarifications as needed. Students should listen respectfully and write down each group's word and brief definition in their vocabulary journals or using the reproducible on page 116.

12. After all words are presented, the class should eliminate duplicates, words already known, and words students do not want to learn.

13. Students should then vote on the final list of words to be learned by the class.

14. The resulting words and their definitions can be written on a fresh copy of the reproducible on page 116, Words Chosen for Vocabulary Self-Collection. The resulting list "focuses on words that students want to learn, that are important to them, and about which they have expressed interest and curiosity" (Ruddell & Shearer, 2002, p. 353).

15. Facilitate further understanding of the words in subsequent class sessions through discussion, Semantic Mapping (see page 102), and other interactive word activities.

Additional Considerations for Successful Implementation

- ♦ Encourage groups to have a backup word to present to the class in case another group takes their chosen word.
- ♦ Limit presentations to about one minute for each word.
- ♦ Discussion leads students to explore word histories, synonyms, and antonyms, and connects the words to their background knowledge and experience.
- ♦ To facilitate the group process, you may need to review and post acceptable behavior and comments regarding group work.

© Tyler Olson, 2014. Under license from Shutterstock, Inc.

References

Haggard, M. R. (1986). The Vocabulary Self-Collection Strategy: Using student interest and world knowledge to enhance vocabulary growth. *Journal of Reading, 29,* 634–642.

Ruddell, M. R., & Shearer, B. A. (2002). "Extraordinary," "tremendous," "exhilarating," "magnificent": Middle school at-risk students become avid word learners with the Vocabulary Self-Collection Strategy (VSS). *Journal of Adolescent and Adult Literacy, 45,* 352–363.

My Personally Selected Vocabulary Words

Title of Text Selection _____

#1 Word Selected _____ Page/Paragraph _____

Sentence Where Word Is Found _____

_____

_____

What I Think It Means _____

_____

_____

Why I Think It Is Important to Learn _____

_____

_____

_____

#2 Word Selected _____ Page/Paragraph _____

Sentence Where Word Is Found _____

_____

_____

What I Think It Means _____

_____

_____

Why I Think It Is Important to Learn _____

_____

_____

_____

Vocabulary Self-Collection Strategy (VSS)

Names of Group Members _____

Title of Selection or Text _____

Word Selected _____ Page/Paragraph _____

Word in Sentence _____

What does the word mean?

_____

_____

_____

_____

_____

We used   _____ Context

           _____ Glossary

           _____ Dictionary

           _____ Internet

           _____ Other

Why we think the word is important to learn.

_____

_____

_____

_____

_____

_____

_____

Words Chosen for Vocabulary Self-Collection

Title of Text or Selection _____

Pages _____

Word	Meaning
1. _____	_____
2. _____	_____
3. _____	_____
4. _____	_____
5. _____	_____
6. _____	_____
7. _____	_____
8. _____	_____

Word Map

Description

A Word Map (Schwartz & Raphael, 1985) is a graphic representation of the definition of a word. The map contains the word, the category to which it belongs, some of its essential characteristics, and some examples. Word Maps help students understand the attributes and characteristics of a word's meaning. A Word Map engages students and encourages them to go beyond just writing a word's definition (a critical aspect of vocabulary learning), as suggested by Beck, McKeown, and Kucan (2013). Due to the time it takes to complete the map, the Word Map graphic organizer should be used for key concept words. It is most effective when used with nouns.

Bridge to the Disciplines

The task of completing a Word Map can encourage students to grapple with how vocabulary is used in a discipline and begin to identify patterns of use. This helps students develop an understanding of how information is created in a discipline and how it is communicated.

Technology Connections

Word Maps can be created using online whiteboard applications like www.bubbl.us or Mindomo (www.mindomo.com); iPad applications can include Explain Everything or Skitch.

Text Type
Narrative
Informational

Disciplinary Considerations
◆ Building specialized vocabulary
◆ Mapping graphic (and mathematical) representations against explanations in the text

Common Core Anchor Standards
Reading
◆ Read closely to determine what the text says explicitly and to make logical inferences from it; cite specific textual evidence . . . drawn from the text.
◆ Read and comprehend complex literary and informational texts.

Language
◆ Determine or clarify the meaning of unknown and multiple-meaning words and phrases by using context clues, analyzing meaningful word parts, and consulting general and specialized reference materials, as appropriate.

Strategic Behaviors
Determining Importance

Suggested Uses for Disciplinary Literacy
ELA: Given an author's name, ask students for characteristics of the author's writing style and examples of selections written.

History: Have students select key conceptual terms like *isolationism* or *urbanization* and provide historical examples. Students can also use categories like *social, political*, or *economic* to organize the terms.

Science: Using a key concept like *continental drift*, ask students to describe it, give examples of the effects of continental drift, and categorize it geologically.

Math: In algebra, provide a key concept word such as *variable*. Characteristics of variables and examples of variables should appear on the maps. Consider student responses carefully and discuss them so that students develop a clear and accurate concept of what a variable is.

Procedure

1. Display the Word Map graphic organizer on page 120. Tell students that this type of map can help them think about what they need to know in order to understand a new word.

2. Model the use of the map by choosing a well-understood concept and inviting the class to participate in completing the map with you. For example, the chosen concept might be "cell phone." Write *cell phone* in the box in the center of the organizer. Ask, "What is it?" Students may respond with *phone* or *mobile phone*. Write one of the responses in the proper place. Then ask, "What makes a cell phone different from other phones?" Properties might include *can send and receive text messages, has games, can play music, can access the Internet*. List these properties in the proper places. Finally, ask students for some examples of cell phones. They may say *Apple iPhone*, *Samsung Galaxy*, and/or *Motorola Droid*. Write these in the appropriate places.

3. Distribute copies of the Word Map reproducible on page 120.

4. Present the key term or concept for the lesson.

5. Invite students to work individually or in pairs to complete the map. Encourage them to use their text and other resources to assist them.

6. When the maps are complete, have students share some of their ideas. When it appears that students clearly understand the key concept, have them write a definition of it, use it in a sentence, and make a picture, image, or association to help them remember it. The definition should include the category of the word, some properties or characteristics, and specific examples.

7. An example from geometry is provided on page 119.

References

Beck, I. L., McKeown, M. G., & Kucan, L. (2013). *Bringing words to life: Robust vocabulary instruction* (2nd ed.). New York, NY: Guilford.

Schwartz, R. M., & Raphael, T. E. (1985). Concept of definition: A key to improving students' vocabulary. *The Reading Teacher, 39,* 198–205.

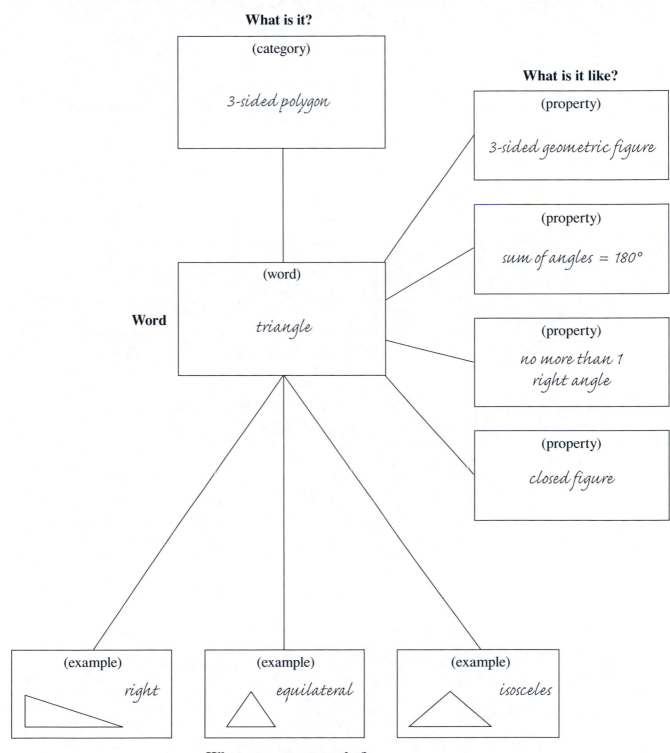

What is it?

(category)

3-sided polygon

What is it like?

(property)

3-sided geometric figure

(property)

sum of angles = 180°

(property)

no more than 1 right angle

(property)

closed figure

Word

(word)

triangle

(example)

right

(example)

equilateral

(example)

isosceles

What are some examples?

Word Map

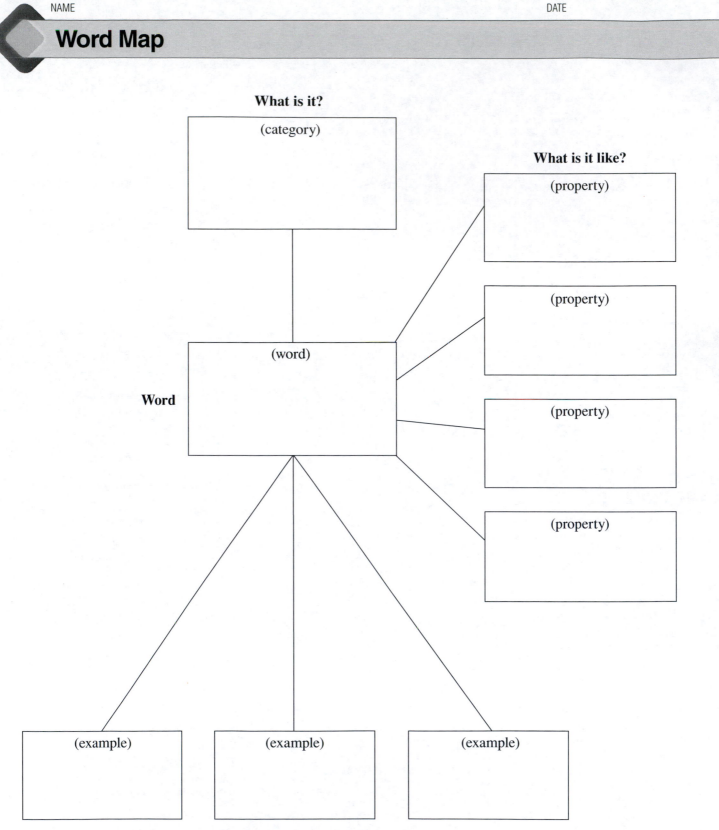

What is it?

(category)

What is it like?

(property)

(property)

Word

(word)

(property)

(property)

(example)   (example)   (example)

What are some examples?

Word Sort

Description

A Word Sort (Templeton, Johnston, Bear, & Invernizzi, 2010) is an activity that engages students in classifying words into categories that make sense to them. Using manipulatives also encourages more interactive group collaboration and discussion. The strategy is derived from Taba's (1967) List-Group-Label strategy and is based on the belief that placing words into categories helps students to organize and remember vocabulary and concepts. There are two types of Word Sorts, Closed and Open, and both involve manipulating words into categories. A Closed Word Sort, which is usually easier, involves moving words into categories that are predetermined and given to students at the outset. In an Open Word Sort, students are invited to consider the characteristics and meanings of the words and then cluster them into categories that students determine. Some of the words in the sort may be used for category headings, or students may create new headings. See examples on page 123. Word Sorts can be used before reading to elicit background knowledge and help set purposes for reading. As a post-reading activity, students consolidate and refine their new learning. Inviting students to sort the same words both before and after reading encourages reflection and refinement of the major concepts of the lesson. This sorting provides a crosschecking experience that can also enhance students' metacognition (awareness of their own learning).

Bridge to the Disciplines

Through the classification process, students grow to understand what information is valued and how it is organized in the discipline. The active process of constructing connections is an important step to building disciplinary knowledge

Technology Connections

This strategy can be done online with a tool called Word Magnets (http://www.triptico.co.uk/index.php). It is particularly effective with SMART Boards.

Text Type
Narrative
Informational

Disciplinary Considerations
◆ Building prior knowledge
◆ Building specialized vocabulary
◆ Mapping graphic (and mathematical) representations against explanations in the text

Common Core Anchor Standards
Reading
◆ Read closely to determine what the text says explicitly and to make logical inferences from it; cite specific textual evidence when writing or speaking to support conclusions drawn from the text.
◆ Interpret words and phrases as they are used in a text, including technical, connotative, and figurative meanings, and analyze how specific word choices shape meaning or tone.

Speaking and Listening
◆ Prepare for and participate effectively in a range of conversations and collaborations with diverse partners.
◆ Integrate and evaluate information.

Language
◆ Determine or clarify the meaning of unknown and multiple-meaning words.

Strategic Behaviors
Using Prior Knowledge
Asking Questions
Inferring
Determining Importance
Synthesizing

Suggested Uses for Disciplinary Literacy
ELA: Create a Word Sort related to the various forms of media and possible effects on society. The resulting classification decisions lead to rich discussion involving critique and corroboration of ideas.

History: When studying civilizations, have students sort words into these given categories: Geography, Religion, Politics, Economics, and Social Structure.

Science: In Earth Science, have students sort names of rocks into categories based on how the rocks are formed.

Math: Invite students to sort terms related to equations, inequalities, and problem solving.

Procedure

1. Select 15–20 vocabulary words that are important for understanding the lesson or unit. Be sure to include some familiar words along with the new words students will be encountering. Decide if you will be asking students to do a Closed or an Open Sort.

2. Write the words on note cards, preparing a set of cards for each small group of students. An alternative is to write the words on the reproducible on page 124, make copies, and have students cut them apart for sorting.

3. Create groups of three to five students, giving each group a set of the note cards containing the vocabulary words. Explain to students that doing a Word Sort is similar to organizing their rooms. When their room is a mess, they can't find anything and may not even know what they have. Ask students to verbally list some of the things in their rooms. Ask them how they find what they need. Hopefully, categories will emerge like shoes, school stuff, jeans, jewelry, and so on. Point out that by grouping their things into categories, they can find what they need when they need it. A Word Sort helps them in the same way. They will understand which words go together and remember them.

4. If it is a Closed Word Sort, provide the categories students should use in clustering the words. If it is an Open Word Sort, tell students to read and discuss the words and then arrange them into categories that make sense to them. Some of the words may become cluster headings and/or they may create headings for their clusters. Students need to be able to defend their classification decisions.

5. Allow students about 10 minutes to complete the sort. Then direct groups to rotate around the classroom, examining how others have clustered the words, or, to save time, have groups share their classifications orally.

6. As students read or experience the lesson, provide opportunities for students to reclassify their words, based on their expanding knowledge of the discipline.

7. At the conclusion of the lesson, invite students to share their reflections. Were their initial classifications correct? Did they make changes? If so, why? Did it increase their understanding of the text?

Additional Considerations for Successful Implementation

- Consider using index cards, sticky notes, or 3x5 slips of paper for the words.

- In an Open Word Sort, provide extra blank cards for students to use to create cluster headings.

- If the activity is done before reading, you may need to provide more support to the groups as they encounter and discuss the words.

- When students finish sorting their words, they can write a summary of the information or a reflection explaining why they chose words for particular categories.

- When students become proficient with Open Sorts, after sharing their categories with the class, have students do another Open Sort with the same words, this time the rule being that they cannot use any category that has already been used. When finished, ask students to share again and discuss their decision processes.

References

Taba, H. (1967). *Teacher's handbook for elementary social studies*. Reading, MA: Addison-Wesley.

Templeton, S., Johnston, F., Bear, D. R., & Invernizzi, M. (2010). *Vocabulary their way: Word study with middle and secondary students*. New York, NY: Pearson.

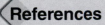

Sample Closed Word Sort for **Social Studies**

Directions: Arrange each of the words below into one of the categories in bold type.

<u>   Anasazi Indians   </u>
(topic)

Who They Were   **What They Did**   **Where They Lived**

ancient ones   nomadic   canyon   invaders   cliff palace

kiva   metates   abode   cliffs   stone masons

hunters   mesa   excavation   swallows   preserve

Sample Open Word Sort for **Science**

Directions: Below are some words that you will find in your lesson. Cut them apart and arrange them in categories according to their meanings. You must be able to justify the reasons for your decisions.

<u>   The Sun   </u>
(topic)

solar flare   solar composition   magnetic storm

solar structure   helium   photosphere

aurora   core   solar wind

atmosphere   hydrogen   sunspot

corona   prominence   chromosphere

solar activities   solar eclipse   nuclear fusion

Word Sort

_____
(topic)

Directions: Below are some words that you will find in your lesson. Cut them apart and arrange them in categories according to their meanings. You must be able to justify the reasons for your decisions.
